Copyright © 2022 Matthew Douglas Pinard

All Rights Reserved. No part of this book publication may be reproduced or transmitted in any form or by any means, mechanical or electronic, including photocopying, scanning, and recording, or by any information storage and retrieval system, or other -- without prior permission in writing from the author or publisher. Disclaimers: The Publisher and the Author make no representation or warranties concerning the accuracy or completeness of the contents of this work and specifically disclaim all warranties for a particular purpose. No warranty may be created or extended through sales or promotional materials. The advice and strategies contained herein may not be suitable for every situation. This work is sold with the understanding that the Author and Publisher are not engaged in rendering legal, technological, or other professional services. If professional assistance is required, the services of a competent professional should be sought. Neither the Publisher nor the Author shall be liable for damages arising therefrom. The fact that an organization or website is referred to in this work as a citation and/or potential source of further information does not mean that the Author or the Publisher endorses the information, the organization, or website it may provide, or recommendations it may make. Further, readers should be aware that the websites listed in this work may have changed or disappeared between the time that this work was written and when it is read. Details of the cases and stories in this book have been changed to preserve privacy.

Printed in the United States of America
Published by: Writer's Publishing House
Prescott, Az 86301

Cover and Interior Design by Creative Artistic Excellence Marketing
Project Management and Book Launch by Creative Artistic Excellence Marketing
https://lizzymcnett.com

Paperback ISBN: 978-1-64873-248-5
Hardcover ISBN: 978-1-64873-249-2
Ebook ISBN: 978-1-64873-251-5

THE NEW WINE: VOLUME IV
KINGDOM COME

Table of Contents

"AND BEHOLD A GREAT RED DRAGON" 5

EARTHQUAKES 19

"A WOMAN CLOTHED WITH THE SUN" 39

Paxton Nathaniel Elkins 44

"THE PARACLETE" 198

"INSANITY'S HORSE ADORNS THE SKY" 207

"THE MARK OF THE BEAST" 239

"OUR FATHER ANNUNAKI ADONAI" 278

"AN ANGELIC APOCALYPSE" 319

Other Books by Author Matthew 409

Screenplay Awards 413

Matthew Douglas Pinard 413

"AND BEHOLD A GREAT RED DRAGON"

    Our Father, who art in Heaven, hallowed be thy name
Thy Kingdom Come, thy will be done, on earth as it is in Heaven
Give us this day, our daily bread, and forgive us our trespasses
As we forgive those who trespass against us and lead us not into
Temptation, but deliver us from evil, for yours is the Kingdom
The power, and the glory, now and forever...Amen

    Since the publication of The New Wine Volume III: The Veil Rent, the apocalyptic events documented in this book have not only continued but also seemed to increase in frequency and magnitude. I decided to write this fourth volume of The New Wine and called it "Kingdom Come." It is my firm belief as both an objective observer of world events and documenter of both natural and supernatural phenomena, as well as a professed and practicing Catholic, that we are definitively in the Book of Revelations.

I will further explain the image on the cover of the book later in detail, but it is definitely an amazing image of Satan being exorcised from this earth. I believe we have, in fact, moved from Chapter 12 with the appearance of Our Mother Mary in the sky as the Woman Clothed in the Sun or The Woman of the Apocalypse, and straight into Chapter 13 where we are now encountering the Red Dragon beast ("behold a red-breasted beast") and his appearance in our skies as seen on the cover of this volume of The New Wine. I will discuss in detail the images on the cover of this volume four of The New Wine later in this book. The image to the left on the cover is Anunnaki Adonai (Our Father who Art in Heaven) and the image to the left is the fallen entity Lucifer/Hillel Ben Shachar/Memnoch/Satan/red dragon/devil/Baphomet.

There is a definitive battle in the spiritual realm, which has a significant impact on our world today. In fact, we recently saw the outbreak of a world pandemic of the lethal coronavirus (COVID-19), and the world response with has nearly paralyzed our economy and changed how we are allowed to interact socially. The goal of this book is not only to document these events but also to hopefully show hope from the divine intervention promised to us on the hill at Calvary with the crucifixion and resurrection.

I recently shared the first two volumes of The New Wine with a Roman Catholic Priest, who is also a noted author, and he stated, "Just from reading these, I can tell you are a Mystic." That has been official validation for me in continuing to publish this series of books with signs and wonders from on high.

I want to take a moment to discuss the Miracle of the Sun at Fatima in 1917. The Fatima apparitions of the Lady of the Rosary (St. Mary) are a widely accepted series of what are termed "miracles of the sun" witnessed by thousands of people in Fatima, Spain during World War I. St. Mary gave a series of apocalyptic visions, and prophecies were given by St. Mary, who appeared floating in a white dress to three farm children named Lucia, Jacinta, and Francisco. There are three "secrets" of Fatima, which all had to do with warnings of wars on Earth, visions of hell, and predictions of a great fire that may befall the entire planet if these warnings were not heeded. The first vision was a glimpse of hell and was described as the following:

"Our Lady showed us a great sea of fire which seemed to be under the earth. Plunged in this fire were demons and souls in human form, like transparent burning embers, all blackened or burnished bronze, floating about in the conflagration, now raised into the air by the flames that issued from within themselves together with great clouds of smoke, now falling back on every side like sparks in a huge fire, without weight or equilibrium, and amid shrieks and groans of pain and despair, which horrified us and made us tremble with fear. The demons could be distinguished by their terrifying and repulsive likeness to frightful and unknown animals, all black and transparent. This vision lasted but an instant."

The second secret of Fatima was a prediction that World War I would end, but that another great war would occur during the reign of Pope Pius XI, and was described as follows:

"You have seen hell where the souls of poor sinners go. To save them, God wishes to establish in the world devotion to my Immaculate Heart. If what I say to you is done, many souls will be saved and there will be peace. The war is going to end: but if people do not cease offending God, a worse one will break out during the Pontificate of Pope Pius XI. When you see a night illumined by an unknown light, know that this is the great sign given you by God that he is about to punish the world for its crimes, utilizing war, famine, and persecutions of the Church and the Holy Father.

"To prevent this, I shall come to ask for the Consecration of Russia to my Immaculate Heart, and the Communion of reparation on the first Saturdays. If my requests are heeded, Russia will be converted, and there will be peace; if not, she will spread her errors throughout the world, causing wars and persecutions of the Church. The goodwill is martyred; the Holy Father will have much to suffer; various nations will be annihilated. In the end, my Immaculate Heart will triumph."

The second secret is fascination from my perspective because it does three powerful things. One accurately predicts the outbreak of World War II, which did occur. Second, it states that the conversion of Russia must be made, or that the threat of a third world war, which will threaten all mankind, will come to fruition. In 2020, this is truer now than ever.

The third is St. Mary states more than once that her "Immaculate Heart" will prevail. Now, this could be mistaken, as her own heart will prevail. However, I believe this is an actual reference to her Son Jesus Christ as the "Immaculate Heart" that prevails. The other interesting part of the secret revelation is a "night illuminated by an unknown light" and this is interesting considering the amazing photographs of miracles of both the sun and light from previous volumes of The New Wine, which all coincidentally began around the one-hundredth anniversary of Fatima in 2017. I believe this fourth volume of The New Wine will also provide many examples of an "unknown light" that "illumines the night." In this instance, I believe the world "night" is not the literal time of the day when we see no light as we sleep, but rather a reference to a world in "the night" due to worship of false idols, materialism, and violence.

The third secret of Fatima was revealed on her death bed of Lucia in 1943, and is fascinating and is described by her as the following vision:

"After the two parts which I have already explained, at the left of Our Lady and a little above, we saw an Angel with a flaming sword in his left hand; flashing, it gave out flames that looked as though they would set the world on fire; but they died out in contact with the splendor that Our Lady radiated towards him from her right hand: pointing to the earth with his right hand, the Angel cried out loud: 'Penance, Penance, Penance, Penance, Penance, Penance, Penance, Penance!' And we saw in an immense light that is God: 'something like how people appear in a mirror when they pass in front of it', a Bishop dressed in White 'we had the impression that it was the Holy Father'.

Other Bishops, Priests, men and women Religious went up a steep mountain, at the top of which there was a big Cross of rough-hewed trunks as of a cork tree with the bark; before reaching there the Holy Father passed through a big city half in ruins and half trembling with halting step, afflicted with pain and sorrow, he prayed for the souls of the corpses he met on his way; having reached the top of the mountain, on his knees at the foot of the big Cross he was killed by a group of soldiers who fired bullets and arrows at him, and in the same way there died one after another the other Bishops, Priests, men and women Religious, and various lay people of different ranks and positions. Beneath the two arms of the Cross, there were two Angels, each with a crystal aspersorium in his hand, in which they gathered up to the blood of the Martyrs and sprinkled the souls that were making their way to God."

The interesting thing about the third secret is that Cardinal Joseph Ratzinger, who would eventually become our Pope, stated, "the purpose of the vision is not to show a film of an irrevocably fixed future. Its meaning is exactly the opposite: it is meant to mobilize the forces of change in the right direction." He claims no revelation of the future is received in this third seal or secret of

Fatima. The one interesting line from this secret or seal I wish to revisit later in this book is the line "an angel with a flaming sword in his left hand." What I do find hopeful with this third seal or secret is the line "sprinkled with souls making their way to God."

Photo: On December 9th, 2019 this volcano erupted on White Island near New Zealand tragically killing 20 people.

Photo: Another amazing sunset near Phoenix, Arizona late 2019 and yet another glimpse of the other kingdom of heaven.

Photo: A very large pyramid shaped UFO in the skies above Washington, D.C. near the pentagon on December 23rd, 2020 the same day we moved west to central Arizona. To me this is the most comforting sight I've ever seen in my life especially after calling in a tip regarding a friend who defected to China and a potential leak or mole in our intelligence agency. To me this picture let me know all my prayers have been answered and the Anunnaki Army has arrived to help stomp out war and destroy actual weapons of mass destruction.

Photo: An incredibly mysterious cloud formation on Christmas Day December 25th, 2019 near the skies above Prescott, Arizona after a local mass celebration.

Photo: Another mysterious looking cloud formation on Christmas Day, December 25th, 2019 in the skies near Prescott, Arizona after a local mass celebration. I definitely see a face or mask in this image.

Photo: This amazing photo was taken sometime in January 2020 and shows what appears to be a very large figure arms outstretched with a rainbow halo around its top.

Photo: This photo was taken in early January 2020 in Salt Lake City, Utah. This is my friend James Falls. I call him "St. James." I met James while traveling on a plane to Utah in May of 2019. James had the courage to talk to me on the plane about his Mormon faith and gave me a copy of the Book of Mormon. After many conversations over dinner we both realized that in spite of our differing religious backgrounds we both basically believe the same thing about God, The other kingdom, and angels and demons.

EARTHQUAKES

On January 7th, 2020, a powerful 6.4 magnitude earthquake struck Puerto Rico and 43 earthquakes followed over two months in addition to a direct hit from a hurricane.

On March 20th, 2020 a 4.5 earthquake struck near Carson City, Nevada. On March 31st, 2020 a 6.5 earthquake, the strongest since 1983, struck near Boise, Idaho and shook many homes and buildings.

On March 25th, 2020 a massive 7.5 earthquake hit the Russian coastline. March 25th is also the Feast of the Annunciation, also known as Lady Day, the Feast of Incarnation, Conception Christi, commemorates the visit of the archangel Gabriel to the Virgin Mary, announcing that she would be the mother of Jesus Christ, Son of God.

On April 4th, 2020, San Diego was shaken by a 4.9 earthquake near a dangerous San Andreas fault-line. There has been at least one earthquake per day of magnitude 4-8 across the planet since the publication of the first volume of The New Wine three years ago.

Photo: The sun setting near Phoenix, Arizona the evening of January 31st, 2020.

Photo: This incredible feather like looking cloud formation appeared on February 20th, 2020 in the skies above Prescott Valley, Arizona.

Photo: In the early afternoon on February 21st, 2020 two white cylindrical unidentified flying objects appeared in the skies above Prescott Valley, Arizona.

These objects created no sound, left no contrail and did not appear to have wings.

Photo: A close up of the white cylindrical unidentified flying object above the skies of Prescott Valley, Arizona on February 21st, 2020. When I see this object the song "The Crystal Ship" by The Doors comes to mind.

Photo: An incredible double rainbow in the skies above our neighborhood on February 22, 2020 as my parents visited from Michigan. The back of my father Bill's head can be seen to the left of the rainbow.

Photo: On February 29th, 2020, this red demonic looking face with horns appeared in the skies above our home near Prescott Valley, Arizona.

If you look closely enough, it has another demonic face near the top right of its forehead. This is a visual example of Lucifer/Hillel Ben Shachar/Memnoch/Satan/red dragon/devil's demonic vine of "lions in the night," and to me also signals the possible birth of the "Anti-Christ," as you see a larger demon controlling a lesser demon in Lucifer.

This is simply this Son of God's opinion, but the Anti-Christ would be a "leader" in technology worth over $100 billion dollars who would deliberately release a deadly virus from one of his "labs" for which only he would have the vaccine. The vaccine itself would also prove deadly to many.

Photo: An amazing photo on the afternoon of February 29th, 2020 near Prescott, Arizona after a hike with my wife Carol. You can see two blue eyes peering through the clouds in the top left of the frame. I call this the "Eyes of God" photo.

Photo: An amazing image taken during a nightly "ghost tour" in Tombstone, Arizona on March 1st, 2020 shows two blue eyes hovering in the bottom left of the frame. This was taken in the Bird Cage Saloon, a place of ill repute where gambling and prostitution were common in the 1800s.

Photo: An incredible image taken from a nightly ghost tour at the Bird Cage Saloon in Tombstone, Arizona on March 1st, 2020. If you look closely enough you can see two faces, one to the left with bald head and one to the right. I showed this image to the owner of the Saloon and he said he definitely sees the ghosts and said they were probably from funerals where this hearse was used to take bodies to the local cemeteries. This is a great example of how a spirit can be present for over one hundred years in the same space not bound by "time."

Photo: An amazing ghostly face the morning of March 6th, 2020 in the skies above Prescott, Arizona after a morning recitation of the rosary at Sacred Heart Catholic Church in Prescott, Arizona.

Photo: In early March 2020 Mt. Merapi in Indonesia erupted sending ash over 16,000 feet into the air.

Photo: An amazing angel cloud wing covering the entire sky near Prescott, Arizona on March 7th, 2020 as I went on a hike in a local mountain area. I believe this is another glimpse of St. Michael the Arch Angel whose incarnate identity was revealed in The New Wine Volume III: The Veil Rent as Michael Hutchence of the rock band INXS. In a recent interview with his bandmates, they all stated they still feel his presence during thunderstorms which would be typical of his influence and presence. In my daily rosary I ask for St. Michael's protection from Lucifer/Hillel Ben Shachar/Memnoch/Satan/red dragon/devil.

Photo: An amazing photo capturing a blue eye orb from the sun on a local hike near Prescott, Arizona on March 7th, 2020.

Photo: Another amazing photo of a blue eye orb from the sun near a local hiking trail near Prescott, Arizona on March 7th, 2020.

Photo: An amazing sunrise the morning of March 9th, 2020 as viewed from Sacred Heart Catholic Church near Prescott, Arizona before a morning rosary.

Photo: The beautiful sunrise the morning of March 12th, 2020 near Denver, Colorado as I traveled to help restore sight working with local retina surgeons.

Photo: Another amazing photo of the sunrise near Denver, Colorado on March 12th, 2020.

Photo: An incredible shot of a very high storm cloud forming above Prescott, Arizona on March 13th, 2020.

Photo: The evening of March 16th, 2020 in the skies above Prescott Valley, Arizona this incredible sunset appeared near our home ushering in Kingdom Come.

Photo: The morning of St. Patrick's Day on March 17th, 2020 this incredible angel cloud formation appeared above Sacred Heart Catholic Church in Prescott, Arizona one day before a major earthquake would strike Salt Lake City, Utah.

Photo: On March 18th, 2020 (two weeks to the day after a work trip to Salt Lake City to work with local retina surgeons to help stomp out blindness) a 5.7 magnitude earthquake struck near downtown Salt Lake City, Utah damaging many buildings and knocking the trumpet off the statue of the Angel Moroni at the top of the Mormon Temple.

Photo: An amazing glimpse of the other kingdom the morning of March 19th, 2020 near Prescott Valley, Arizona. Notice the odd blue orb below the crack in the clouds giving yet another glimpse of the other kingdom.

Photo: An amazing angelic cloud formation in the skies above Prescott, Arizona on March 21st, 2020. I showed this photo to a relative who is a devout Catholic and he said, "Father, Son, and Holy Ghost."

Photo: Another amazing and mystical looking cloud formation on March 21st, 2020 near Prescott Valley, Arizona.

"A WOMAN CLOTHED WITH THE SUN"

As I described in the first three volumes of The New Wine, the incredible prophecy of a "woman who will appear clothed with the sun" from 95 A.D., describes the events leading to St. Mary, the mother of Jesus Christ appearing at a time signaling the apocalypse.

The prophecy describes a woman giving birth to a male child threatened by a dragon, identified as the Devil or Satan, who intends to devour the child as soon as he is born. When the child is taken to heaven, the woman flees into the wilderness, leading to a "war in heaven" in which the angels cast out the dragon.

The dragon then attacks the woman, who is given wings to escape, and then attacks her again with a flood of water from his mouth, which is then swallowed by the earth. Frustrated, the dragon initiates war on the "remnant of her seed" identified as the righteous followers of Christ.

As I will show in this chapter, I believe the child referenced in this prophecy is young Paxton Nathaniel Elkins. Paxton was first introduced in the first volume of The New Wine and waged a courageous battle against terminal brain stem cancer. Before his death, he told family that a blonde man came into his bedroom to tell him he was going to heaven and would have his mansion with all the My Little Ponies he wanted.

When Paxton finally passed away, he was not on a respirator, as the doctors said he would be, and lived six months past most children with this diagnosis. At his gravesite, during his funeral, a pair of large angel wings appeared in the sky. Although Paxton died at age 8 and not "as soon as he was born", as this prophecy states, there is something else to consider as to this meaning.

Paxton's family told me he had never been baptized or given first communion so he wasn't "born into Christ" yet. As we saw in The New Wine Volumes III, there were multiple photos of the red dragon in that volume, as there are in this volume. This volume of The New Wine also has incredible photos, as I will show later of angels and demons in a "war in heaven."

We are also seeing definitive attacks on righteous followers of Christ, as the coronavirus has led to the closing of places of worship.

Photo: An amazing image of very apocalyptic looking clouds lit by the setting sun in the skies above Prescott Valley, Arizona the evening of March 21st, 2020. Just as these mysterious looking clouds appeared an incredible light green orb appeared which I will show in the next image.

Photo: An incredible shot of the sun setting on March 21st, 2020. Of particular interest is the red halo and a very oddly shaped green orb. What is also amazing about this green orb as I will show in another photo below, a similar orb was found in a photo of the sun setting near Lake Michigan in 2017 as I prayed for the life of young Paxton Elkins who courageously was fighting terminal brain cancer.

Photo: A mysterious "floating" green orb on the waves of Lake Michigan as I prayed for the life of young Paxton Elkins who was fighting terminal brain cancer.

Paxton Nathaniel Elkins

Allow me to take a moment to convey what I believe this amazing green orb could possibly be. During every morning, I say at least one full rosary, asking St. Mary to bring back Paxton Nathaniel Elkins to this world. If you have read any of my previous three volumes of The New Wine, you will recall Paxton, who was seven years old when I first met him and his family shortly after he was diagnosed by one of my ophthalmic surgeons with terminal DIPG (diffuse intrinsic pontine glioma).

I had a profound sense from St. Mary that I was to do everything in my earthly power to save his life (even if it meant losing mine). Paxton and I prayed together in the presence of his family at St. Paul Catholic Church in Valparaiso, IN for God the Father to take his disease from his brain and, if necessary, move the cancer into mine. I have never shared this publicly, but during this time I started receiving inexplicable headaches and dizziness, while Paxton seemed to improve his energy.

In fact, he lived six months past the date 97% of children diagnosed with DIPG passed away. His mother stated to me that he kept saying "Jesus will heal my bump."

During my daily prayers, I ask St. Mary to send Paxton back "seven times" and to "scatter that Son."

What I mean by this is would it not be an amazing feat of Our Father in Heaven to bring seven newborns to this world that look like they were born to seven different families, and that when each of these children is seven, they start remembering praying with Jesus in a Catholic church to heal "their bump."

Will this happen? I do not know; however, I do know, it could happen, and if this did, would that be proof enough for every world leader to disarm weapons of mass destruction and turn away from greed.

The night of March 23d, 2020 a fireball meteor lit up the night sky above northern Florida. Two similar meteor fireballs were recorded earlier in the year near my home in Prescott, Arizona, one of them on the exact date of my birthday, February 26th, 2020.

Headline news on March 31st, 2020 read "biggest asteroid to approach in April 2020, arriving next week NASA reveals." The article describes the asteroid as big as the Empire State Building, with a diameter of 1,248 feet moving at Earth at a speed of 55,000 mph, and based on its size and speed, it could cause a major impact event on Earth that would leave a crater four miles wide and create blast waves that could destroy an entire city.

On March 5th, 2020, deadly tornadoes killed 25 people in Nashville, Tennessee. On March 31st, 2020, several powerful tornadoes touched down near Tallahassee, Florida.

Photo: _The Elkins family of Portage, Indiana. Paxton (far right) is pictured here with his fraternal twin Landon during the summer of 2017 as young Paxton put up a courageous fight against terminal brain cancer. I truly believe God has a beautiful plan for this family that has not yet unfolded.

I will convey here an amazing story that happened shortly after he passed away. Days before he died, Paxton stated a blonde man (who he identified as Jesus) came into his room to tell him he was getting his own mansion in heaven with all my little ponies he wanted.

I believe Paxton was actually visited by Arch Angel Gabriel, who is blonde. A few days after Paxton's funeral, I told his mother Krista that this was definitely not the last time we heard from Paxton. Krista, to her credit in a feat of amazing spirit, sent me an incredible video a few days later.

In the video, people can be seen getting buzzed haircuts in a bar in solidarity for cancer patients. Incredibly in the background near one of the windows, just as Paxton's name was called out, a bright ray of light can be seen cracking through the window pane and illuminating the top of one of the girl's shaved head.

Photo: _The folded Arch Angel wings of St. Gabriel appear directly above the gravesite of Paxton Nathaniel Elkins after his funeral in the fall of 2017 following a battle with DIPG brain cancer. There is no doubt in my mind he is flying with the angels in heaven and on earth. I do believe that one day he will return as our incarnate scattered sun king.

In the prophecy of "The Woman Clothed in the Sun", it states that a child is taken up into heaven as the Great Red Dragon wages war against the woman clothed in the sun and her remnants on earth.

I firmly believe this child is young Paxton Nathaniel Elkins for many reasons. First, he was a fraternal twin, and St. Mary uses fraternal twins presently to confuse the Great Red Dragon (Lucifer) and his lions of the night (demons).

The other reason I believe this is because St. Mary appeared in an apparition to me right before I met Paxton and his family in early 2017. The other reason is that as we prayed for him, many "paranormal events" began to unfold.

The first was the appearance of the Holy Spirit in the sky in West Michigan as we prayed for Paxton. The other amazing thing that happened, as documented in the first volume of The New Wine, was the earthquake in Pakistan in the tropic of cancer. The very minute the white winged dove (shown below) appeared above Lake Michigan.

Photo: This incredible image of the "Paraclete" the Holy Spirit in natural form diving headfirst toward Portage, Indiana as it appeared on February 8th, 2017 above Lake Michigan. The exact moment this image appeared an earthquake struck in the tropic of cancer near Pakistan. As I mentioned Pakistan is very close phonetically to Paxton. Since the appearance of the paraclete (advocate) white winged dove major apocalyptic events have occurred on our planet in the form of earthquakes, volcanoes, hurricanes, tornadoes, meteors and floods have ravaged the planet.

Photo: Another Jim Morrison prophesy come true, a "self-crowning sun" as seen in the first volume of The New Wine in the fall of 2016 near Grand Haven, Michigan or as Jim prophesied in the song "Texas Radio and the Big Beat/Love Me Two Times" by singing, "and one morning you awoke, and the strange sun, and opening your door."

Photo: The New Wine and The New Rose standing on a rock near Grand Haven Pier in Grand Haven, Michigan in the fall of 2016. I am going to now decode prophetic lyrics from the song "Set It Off" by the band Audioslave as written and performed by the prophet Chris Cornell. In the song he sings "he was standing at the rock, gathering the flock, getting there with no directions." This prophetic song then goes on to say, "every time the wind blows, everything you don't know turns into a revelation." This incredible line also is marking that when these events would occur we would be in the Book of Revelations and that when the gates would be opened and the strange sun would appear that I would be on a rock to witness the beginning of the apocalypse.

Photo: This incredible image is from September 5th, 2017 near Grand Haven State Park in West Michigan. This incredible image taken by my wife Carol Rose shows what appears to be twin suns in the sky, or two suns.

I believe the star or sun to the right is Nibiru and is also the Prophet Chris Cornell's "Black Hole Sun," as revealed in the song of the same name written and performed by his band Soundgarden, as well as Gordon Sumner's (Sting) "Invisible Sun."

According to scientists, most universes thought to host life would be a binary star system, and it is possible to have an "invisible" sun that would emit light at bands that would only be perceived under certain conditions.

In his song "Black Hole Sun," Chris Cornell sings, "Black Hole Sun, won't you come and wash away the rain?" I believe Chris "foresaw" the appearance of this "black hole sun" that would wipe away sorrow and suffering.

I find it ironic that Chris died in Michigan just a few months before this "invisible sun" made its appearance in West Michigan.

When asked what the lyrics of Black Hole Sun were about, Chris Cornell stated, "A black hole is a billion times larger than a sun, it's a void, a giant circle of nothing, and then you have the sun, the giver of all life. It was this combination of bright and dark, this sense of hope and underlying moodiness."

Photo: This incredible photo was taken on February 9th, 2017 by the mother of young Paxton Nathaniel Elkins, who had recently been diagnosed with terminal brain cancer. That is remarkable about this photo is the green orb to the left near the base of his brain where his cancer was, in addition to the sun's rays hitting his face in the middle of winter in the Midwest.

Three days before this photo was taken, Paxton and I touched hands at St. Paul's Catholic Church in Valparaiso, Indiana, and said three Hail Mary's asking God to take away the cancer from his brain. Paxton lived six months before doctors said he should have, and died at age eight after telling us Jesus was going to heal his "bump" in his brain. By the time Paxton died, experts in brain tumors (including my cousin, who is a neurosurgeon) said he should have been on a breathing tube.

A few days before he died, Paxton stated a blonde man was visiting him and telling him he was going to get his own mansion in heaven with all my little ponies he wanted. I asked his mother how he was the days before his death, and she said he was in absolutely no pain whatsoever and running around the house fairly carefree.

Photo: The large wings of Arch Angel Gabriel that appeared at the funeral of young Paxton Elkins of Portage, Indiana in the fall of 2017. This image is also a prophecy from the Audioslave song "Set It Off" where the prophet Chris Cornell sings "and underneath the Arch (Gabriel) it turned into a march, and there he got the spark to set this fucker off (Apocalypse)."

Photo: The image of St. Mary "clothed with the sun" as shown in the first three volumes of The New Wine. This image was taken at a Chicago toll booth as I drove the day after Christmas 2016 to pray with the dying mother of a good friend. I am going to now decode St. Michael (Hutchence) and his song "Mystify Me" as recorded by the band INXS. In this song St. Michael sings "all veils and misty, streets of blue, almond looks that chill divine, some silken moment goes on forever and we're leaving broken hearts behind." Here is is prophesying this very moment when St. Mary would appear thus "leaving broken hearts behind" for those that embrace her and her fraternal twin sons.

Photo: This incredibly beautiful painting of St. Mary inside St. Germaine Catholic Church in Prescott Valley, Arizona shows the Virgin of Guadalupe standing above or on top of Lucifer/Hillel Ben Shachar/Memnoch/Satan/red dragon/devil/baphomet demonstrating she has full spiritual authority over the dark one.

Photo: A print of the famous William Blake painting "The Great Red Dragon and the Woman Clothed in the Sun" is itself a painted prophecy accurately predicting the appearance of St. Mary clothed in the sun (see previous photo) at a time of great turmoil in the world.

"And behold a great red dragon, having seven heads and ten horns, and seven crowns upon his head. And his tail drew the third part of the stars of heaven, and did cast them to the earth." - Revelations 12:3-4, KJV

This prophecy from the Book of Revelations is depicted by the William Blake painting "The Great Red Dragon and the Woman Clothed in the Sun" and informs us all that we are currently in the Book of Revelations.

Events in the world are indicative of this truth. For example, since publication of The New Wine Volume I, there has been a major earthquake of magnitude 4-8 on the Richter scale every day (trust me, I have tracked this daily). In addition, we have nations rising up against other nations. Currently, North Korea and South Korea are exchanging gunfire on the DMZ.

China may have already initiated the release of a bioweapon in COVID-19, and Russia has threatened nuclear war over proxy skirmishes in Middle Eastern countries. The United States Secretary of Defense publicly stated he was dedicating military resources in the South China Seas to thwart Chinese expansion and aggression, and recently a fleet of U.S. Navy ships were seen entering the South Pacific with "long range missiles."

We are seeing inordinate displays of greed, as billionaires have dramatically increased, and the middle class in America is all but extinct. 50% of all Americans live paycheck to paycheck.

The outbreak of the coronavirus has created over six million unemployment claims. Prison populations are increasing, and mass shootings at schools and churches are at an all-time record high. It is safe to say the "Great Red Dragon", also known as Lucifer/Hillel

Ben Shachar/Memnoch/Satan/red dragon/devil, who has now shown in face in multiple photographs in the last two volumes of The New Wine (The Veil Rent and Kingdom Come), needs some restraint.

At present, my daily prayers are asking for my Arch Angels to lead him back to Heaven/Eden, the other kingdom, to face Our Father before he does something to this planet. No human being will survive. His imprint can be seen among Hollywood celebrities.

In fact, my wife and I recently watched a Jennifer Lopez movie in which one of the characters mockingly professed in a line of dialogue "what the people want is to work underground." This line came across as odd in the middle of what was supposed to be a comedy film. A scene then followed this scene, showing a pack of white winged doves released by Jennifer Lopez's character, only to watch them fly into an oncoming delivery truck to be killed instantly.

To me, this was a mocking of God's command that peace be on earth and no more wars be waged. We are living in a very dangerous and life changing time for every human being and living creature here on earth.

I want to know enclose two photos that, in my opinion, are simply amazing. The first is from The New Wine Volume II: Peace Town, and it shows the "choir of angels" that appeared above the beaches of Lake Michigan in the summer of 2017 as I prayed fervently for the life of Paxton Elkins who was diagnosed with terminal brain cancer.

The second photo is another "choir of angels" that appeared directly above my home near Prescott Valley, Arizona almost exactly three years later in May of 2020. The similarities are undeniable.

Photo: The "choir of angels" photo from the summer of 2017 as I prayed for the life of young Paxton Elkins of Portage, Indiana who had recently been diagnosed with terminal brain cancer. This amazing photo of angels appeared above the beaches of Lake Michigan near our home in Grand Haven, Michigan.

Photo: A second "choir of angels" appeared directly over our subdivision near Prescott Valley, Arizona on May 21st, 2020 almost exactly three years after an almost identical formation was photographed in west Michigan near our home.

Photo: The sunset the night of May 21st, 2020 near our home in Prescott Valley, Arizona in an amazing display of true king authority in nature. You can clearly see an angel wing to the right and a very clear green orb above the sun surrounded by a purple haze or halo. The very minute this appeared in our skies the song "What you Need" by INXS as sung by St. Michael Hutchence came on the radio.

Photo: A beautiful sunrise with red orb the morning of March 23rd, 2020 near our home in Prescott Valley, Arizona.

Photo: An outside grotto with a statue of St. Mary at St. Catherine Catholic Church in nearby Chino Valley, Arizona on March 27th, 2020 as a new pandemic hit the globe. I pray my rosary, since many churches are closed due to the recent outbreak of the COVID-19 coronavirus, which has killed thousands worldwide.

Allow me to decode a bit more of Jim Morrison's prophetic lyrics while performing with The Doors.

In the song "When the Music's Over", he sings "a feast of friends, alive she cried, waiting for me outside."

He saw us both praying here at this grotto "outside" years before it was made. Jim was both prophet and incarnate Son of God and the other half of my spirit.

We are the twin Sons of Mary that are "revved up like a deuce, another runner in the night" as prophesied by Bruce Springsteen and Manfred Mann.

Photo: On March 28th, 2020 this very mysterious cloud appeared above our home near Prescott Valley, Arizona.

Photo: An amazing photo of the setting sun on March 28th, 2020 near Prescott Valley, Arizona.

Photo: An incredible sunrise the early morning of March 31st, 2020 above Sacred Heart Catholic Church in Prescott, Arizona. The mix of red and orange hues is simply breathtaking. Jim Morrison, lead singer of The Doors, used to prophesy this moment saying "give a hundred hues, a rich mandala for me and you" knowing we would be together in 2020.

On April 1st, 2020 headlines read rare ocean storms to bring heavy wind and rain to New England and could rival in characteristic the same intensity of the "perfect storm" of 1991, where a Nor Easter collided with a hurricane to force waves over one hundred feet high from hurricane-force winds.

On April 2nd, 2020 headlines read "fireball explodes over the United Kingdom in 'amazing' display." A second "supermoon" made a worldwide appearance in April 2020, as well as two major storms set to batter the west coast with 45 to 90 mph winds, heavy rain, and snow.

On April 6th, 2020 headlines read "mudslide in Hollywood Hills as storm lashes Southern California with rain" as more rain fell on southern California in twenty-four hours than the total recorded for April in that region in history, as more than a foot and a half of snow also fell on mountains surrounding Los Angeles.

Also, on April 6th, 2020, Japan's Mt. Sakurajima erupted, sending ash into the sky, which was preceded by the volcano eruption in late 2019 that killed 20 people in New Zealand, and the eruption of Mt. Merapi in Indonesia in March 2020.

Also, on April 6th, 2020, a category 5 cyclone named Harold, one of the largest ever recorded in the South Pacific, hit the island of Vanuatu.

On April 7th, 2020, nearly 50,000 homes lost power as major storms hit Pennsylvania and dropped hail the entire way as it moved from Ohio to Virginia. There were 33 large golf ball sized hail reports across Michigan the same day.

On April 8th, 2020, a 5.4 earthquake struck near Fiji in the South Pacific Ocean. Also, on April 8th, 2020, the steamboat geyser at Yellowstone "burst into life" recording over 111 small earthquakes, as odd videos of thousands of birds circling near West Virginia were seen on YouTube, leading some to speculate a major change in climate and/or a predictor of a major natural disaster hitting.

Also on April 8th, 2020, six tornadoes touched down in Ohio. On April 10th, 2020, over 51,600 homes were left without power as a rare April snowstorm hit Maine.

On April 10th, 2020, the volcano at Krakatoa in Indonesia erupted, shooting ash 15 km into the sky as people in Jakarta heard a loud boom 150 km away.

On April 11th, 2020 a magnitude 5.2 earthquake struck near Bodie, California near the Nevada border and a 5.1 magnitude earthquake hit Japan.

On Easter Sunday, April 12th, 2020, more than 13 tornadoes ripped through Arkansas, Mississippi, and Louisiana, causing major damage. This put over 95 million people in harm's way while dropping tennis ball sized hail along the way. In this same storm, two EF5 tornadoes touched down simultaneously (an event never before recorded), killing 20 people and leaving 1.3 million homes without power.

On April 15th, 2020, a magnitude 5.7 earthquake hit Columbia, a magnitude 5.6 earthquake hit Indonesia, and a magnitude 5.3 hit Papua New Guinea all on the same day.

On April 16th, 2020, a 6.0 magnitude earthquake hit Honduras, while a 5.9 magnitude earthquake hit Myanmar.

On April 18th, 2020, a 6.6 magnitude earthquake struck near the coast of Japan.

On April 19th, 2020, a second 6.2 magnitude earthquake struck again near the coast of Japan. Also on April 19th, 2020, the Rincon de la Vieja volcano erupted in Costa Rica, sending ash 1.5 km into the air.

On April 21st, 2020, Mt. Etna erupted, sending ash 5 km into the sky as tornadoes continued to ravage the southeastern United States. Also on April 21st, 2020, a 5.3 magnitude earthquake struck near the coast of Japan.

On April 22nd, 2020 (Earth Day), a 5.5 magnitude earthquake struck Tonga, and another 5.2 magnitude earthquake struck the mainland of Japan. Also on April 22nd, 2020, a magnitude 3.7 earthquake struck near Los Angeles, CA.

On April 23rd, 2020, a 5.2 magnitude earthquake struck Japan again, as two 5.5 magnitude earthquakes struck near Mexico and Chile. On April 24th, 2020, severe storms and tornadoes killed people in Texas, Oklahoma, and Florida as a 6.2 magnitude earthquake hit Papau, New Guinea.

Also, on April 24th, 2020, the Sakurajima volcano in Japan erupted flinging lava bombs and ash 11,000 feet into the air as 26 earthquakes struck nearby. Just as I was hiking near a local

Prescott, Arizona memorial to fallen "hot shots" who died after fighting a raging forest fire near Yarnell, Arizona in 2013.

On April 25th, 2020, a 4.9 magnitude earthquake struck Japan, as a 5.2 magnitude earthquake struck near Papua New Guinea on April 26th, 2020.

On April 26th a magnitude 4.0 earthquake struck near Ridgecrest, California threatening to create a dangerous mudslide.

On April 27th, 2020, a magnitude 5.4 earthquake struck again near Papua New Guinea, as dangerous rain, storms, and wind threaten to hit the northeastern United States for the last few days of April 2020.

Also on April 27th, 2020, a 5.6 magnitude earthquake struck New Zealand, the strongest earthquake of 2020 for that region, as the tallest volcano in Eurasia erupted, sending ash 7,000 meters into the air in Russia's far east. On April 28th, 2020 headlines read, "severe storms are likely from Austin to Chicago."

On April 28th, 2020, a magnitude 5.4 earthquake struck Argentina, and on April 29th, 2020, a magnitude 6.6 earthquake struck Cuba, as another 5.2 magnitude earthquake struck near Japan.

On April 29th, 2020, a mile wide asteroid passed by Earth at a safe but close distance. Many online "conspiracy theorists" have postulated that this asteroid is an alien craft after receiving "visions from God." The month of April 2020 also saw over 140 earthquakes hit the super caldera at Yellowstone National Park.

On April 30th, 2020, a 5.4 magnitude earthquake struck Chile. Also, on April 30th, 2020 headlines read "Russian volcano Ebeko sparks 'apocalyptic' panic after submerging entire city in ash," and a 6.1 magnitude earthquake struck the Philippines, killing eight people.

Photo: An apocalyptic hail storm closing in on downtown Seattle on April 1st, 2020.

Photo: An amazing angel wing cloud formation directly above our home near Prescott Valley, Arizona on April 1st, 2020. This appeared as I began writing this fourth volume of The New Wine.

Photo: Mt. Sakurajima in Japan erupted sending ash high into the air on April 6th, 2020.

Photo: A very powerful and fast moving thunderstorm system moved from Ohio to Virginia on April 7th, 2020 and dropped golf ball sized hail the entire way as it traveled 250 miles in eight hours.

Photo: A very large and very bright supermoon in the skies at dusk near the mountains surrounding Prescott Valley, Arizona on April 7th, 2020.

Photo: An amazing sunrise the morning of April 8th, 2020 near Prescott Valley, Arizona while on the way to do a rosary at Sacred Heart Catholic Church in Prescott, Arizona.

Photo: On April 9th, 2020 the Shiveluch volcano erupted in Russia sending ash 10 kilometers into the sky.

Photo: An amazing shot of the other kingdom, a SunDome, with beautiful multi- colored orb present above our new home near Prescott Valley, Arizona on April 10th, 2020.

Photo: Another mysterious angel wing cloud forming over Prescott Valley, Arizona on April 10th, 2020.

Photo: Another amazing angel cloud forming near Prescott Valley, Arizona on April 10th, 2020.

Photo: The morning of April 11th, 2020 this beautiful sunset lit up the skies near Prescott Valley, Arizona while on my way to do a rosary for world peace and for the world to turn away from idolatry and greed.

Photo: The sun behind a cloud giving us another glimpse of the other kingdom the morning of April 11th, 2020 while driving home from Sacred Heart Catholic Church near Prescott, Arizona.

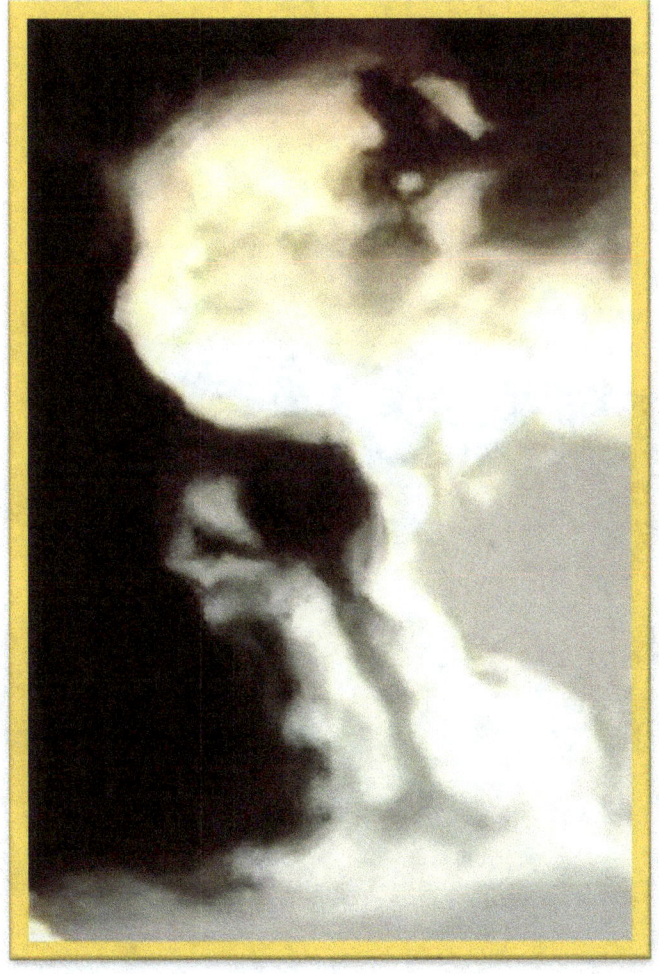

Photo: A blow up of an image of a cloud at sunset on April 11th, 2020 reveals an incredible silhouette of a woman with long braided hair looking to the left and smiling. This image was discovered by my wife Carol Rose Kloss (The New Rose) one day before Easter Sunday from one of my photos I had taken after a rosary at Sacred Heart Catholic Church in Prescott, Arizona. When I showed this photo to a relative who is a devout Catholic he said, "Mary is rejoicing that her Lord has risen."

Photo: An amazing glimpse of the other kingdom and "God's pillow" directly above Sacred Heart Catholic Church after a recitation of the full rosary on April 11th, 2020.

Photo: More heavenly clouds and a glimpse of the other kingdom from April 11th, 2020.

Photo: The evening of Easter Sunday, April 12th, 2020 revealed a very mysterious image in the clouds that appeared to both my wife Carol and I as a large crystal skull alien like head with dark eyes, nose and mouth in the middle of the frame. This image appeared as major storms battered the southern United States.

Photo: A very large and dangerous tornado touches down on Easter Sunday, April 12th, 2020 in Mississippi. This storm was noted for having two F5 tornadoes touch down at the same time.

Photo: An Icelandic volcano erupting underneath the northern lights. In April 2020 this region saw a "dramatic increase" in volcanic activity that could "cause disruption for centuries" according to scientists.

Photo: An acrylic painting I completed the day after Easter Sunday on April 13th, 2020 based on a photo of the red rocks of Sedona, Arizona, a very spiritual and mystical place thought to be frequented by alien life.

Photo: The morning of April 14th, 2020 shows a beautiful cloud layer reflecting the morning sunrise on my way to Sacred Heart Catholic Church in Prescott, Arizona for a morning rosary for world peace and for the world to turn away from idolatry and greed.

On April 14th, 2020 headlines read, "timing of large earthquakes follows a 'devil's staircase' pattern."

The article claims that large shallow earthquakes seem to follow a mathematical pattern known as the 'devil's staircase'. 'The devil's staircase, which is a Cantor function, is a fractal demonstrated by nonlinear dynamic systems in which a change in any part could affect the dynamic of the whole system.

The devil's staircase was discovered during a temporal study of the neuronal patterns of a notorious serial killer brain patterns who killed 52 people from 1979 to 1990. The "timing" of his killings was a 'devil's staircase' pattern. The pattern is also present in earthquake studies, where fault rupture could stimulate activity on other faults by stress transfer.

I find this very scientific explanation of natural phenomena like earthquakes relevant to spiritual attacks of the devil. For example, a change in any soul that allows the devil to enter their spirit and take control can have a major effect on the system as a whole. For example, a tyrannical dictator threatening nuclear war on Earth, or a single man worth over $100 billion that helps no one but themselves with that overabundance of resources, can have major effects on society and the Body of Christ as a whole.

The vine of Satan is unpredictable and elusive and can affect major events on earth. Satan is also adept at "assigning" lesser entities to subdue and control human beings (the band Queen's lyric "Beelzebub has a devil put aside for me" comes to mind) and thus a similar spiritual "stress transfer" as along a fault line that can lead to major "eruptions" of violence or war.

The morning of April 14th, 2020, I visited Sacred Heart Catholic Church in Prescott, Arizona to do two full rosaries. I asked St. Mary to heal this world of disease (COVID-19), greed, and war, and to use Anunnaki angel to drive out demons from the earth. As I walked out of the church, I had an intuition to turn around and look at the sky directly above the church.

What I saw and photographed is simply beyond words. Very clearly in the sky formed as clouds were an angel dragging a demon behind it, with a large wing separating the two. I will attach photos of this phenomenon below.

Photo: A large angel flying above Sacred Heart Catholic Church near Prescott, Arizona the morning of April 14th, 2020, larger wing is seen behind the angel in flight pulling or dragging a demon behind it. I showed this image to Sacred Heart Priest Father Raj Britto who concurred that is indeed an angel in flight.

Photo: Close up shot of the angel in flight above Sacred Heart Catholic Church in Prescott, Arizona on April 14th, 2020 after two rosaries asking St. Mary to drive demons off of the earth.

Photo: A large angel wing pulling or dragging a demonic looking figure behind it off of the earth on April 14th, 2020 at Sacred Heart Catholic Church in Prescott, Arizona.

Photo: A close up of the demon's face is shown here as it is being pulled or dragged by a much larger angel. You can clearly see two horns, two eyes, and a mouth open with tongue sticking out. This image appeared the morning of April 14th, 2020 after two rosaries at Sacred Heart Catholic Church in Prescott, Arizona.

Photo: An acrylic painting I completed on April 15th, 2020 of a white buffalo on Devil's bridge in Sedona, Arizona. The white buffalo is considered sacred by many native American tribes and a symbol of spiritual rebirth.

Photo: The morning of April 17th, 2020 after a full rosary at Sacred Heart Catholic Church in Prescott, Arizona asking St. Mary to protect me from Lucifer/Hillel Ben Shachar/Memnoch/Satan/red dragon/devil with Arch Angel St. Michael's wing this image appeared directly above our home in Prescott Valley, Arizona.

Photo: Another amazing angel cloud wing in the skies above Prescott Valley, Arizona on April 17th, 2020 after a morning rosary at Sacred Heart Catholic Church in Prescott, Arizona for world peace and for the world to turn away from idolatry and greed.

Photo: The morning of April 17th, 2020 this "lion cub face" cloud formed directly above our home near Prescott Valley, Arizona after a full rosary recitation at Sacred Heart Catholic Church asking for protection from Lucifer/ Hillel Ben Shachar/Memnoch/Satan/red dragon/devil and his "lions of the night."

Photo: While on a midafternoon on April 19th, 2020 hike near Prescott Valley, Arizona I took this photo of what appears to be a white rabbit head in the clouds. This image immediately brought to mind the lyrics from one of my favorite songs "White Rabbit" by Jefferson Airplane, "and if you go chasing rabbits, and you know you're going to fall."

Photo: An ominous looking skull like face with two winged horns on top of its head taken while on a walk near Prescott Valley, Arizona on April 19th, 2020. If you look closely enough you can see a face within the face of the skeleton.

Photo: Another ominous looking face with horns in the clouds above Prescott Valley, Arizona on April 19th, 2020.

Photo: Another demonic looking face in the clouds above Prescott Valley, Arizona on April 19th, 2020 as more violent storms were set to hit the southeastern United States.

Photo: Lightning strike on Sunday, April 19th, 2020 near Houston, Texas as strong storms producing lightning and tornadoes moves across the Southeast United States exactly one week after the Easter Sunday tornado outbreak that killed 20 people.

Photo: A powerful and fast-moving storm in New Jersey on April 20th, 2020 ripped down power lines and trees. If you look closely enough you can see what appears as two demonic faces in the cloud.

Photo: The new sun over Prescott, Arizona the morning of April 24th, 2020 while hiking near a memorial to fallen "hot shot" firefighters near Thumb Butte. Notice the halo around the sun and the green orb below in the middle of the frame.

Photo: Thumb Butte hiking trail on April 24th, 2020 near a memorial to the fallen "hot shot" firefighters who died fighting the Yarnell Hill fire of 2013.

Photo: A memorial the fallen 19 "hot shot" firefighters who died in 2013 while fighting the Yarnell Hill wildfire of 2013 as photographed during a hike on April 24th, 2020 near Thumb Butte in Prescott, Arizona. This event was memorialized in the motion picture "Only The Brave" starring Anunnaki Angel half breeds Josh Brolin, Jeff Bridges, and Jennifer Connelly. Moments after visiting this memorial and asking the fallen 19 firefighters to enter my father's kingdom the Sakurajima volcano in Japan erupted ejecting "lava bombs" and ash 11,000 feet into the air.

Photo: On April 25th, 2020 this very mysterious cloud formed above our home near Prescott Valley, Arizona. I clearly see what looks like an alien face with large eyes.

Photo: An amazing image the morning of April 26th, 2020 after a full rosary asking for St. Mary to use our Arch Angels to drive Lucifer/Hillel Ben Shachar/ Memnoch/Satan/red dragon/devil off of the earth this image of a very large "goat" appeared in the sky. Lucifer is often depicted as a goat in mythology.

Photo: On April 25th, 2020 a major storm producing baseball sized hail and lightning struck near Bossier Parish, Louisiana with this amazing display of God's awesome power.

Photo: A very demonic looking skull appeared in the skies above Prescott Valley, Arizona on April 26th, 2020.

Photo: A very demonic looking face appeared in the skies above Prescott Valley, Arizona on April 26th, 2020.

Photo: A very odd shaped alien like head with large eyes appeared in the skies above Prescott Valley, Arizona on April 26th, 2020.

Photo: The morning of April 28th, 2020 in the skies near Prescott Valley, Arizona this sunrise appeared after a morning rosary outside St. Catherine Catholic Church in Chino Valley, Arizona. I asked during my rosary for this world to turn away from war and greed, to heal the victims of COVID-19 and hold those responsible for its release. I also asked for a beautiful sunrise to let me know my prayers were heard, and for the world to hear St. Mary's Son sing again live at least one more time. Just as this sunrise appeared I had an intuition to turn on the radio and change the channel, as I did the Doors song "L.A. Woman" came on. I definitely see an all-seeing eye in the middle of the frame here.

Photo: On the morning of April 28th, 2020 this very demonic "lion of the night" face appeared near the bottom left of the frame following a morning rosary asking St. Mary to drive out evil from this world that takes the form of war and greed.

Photo: On April 28th, 2020 this very mysterious cloud appeared above our home near Prescott Valley, Arizona. If you look closely enough to the top right you can see a male angel with his wings folded behind his back and his chest sticking out. I did not ask him his name, unfortunately, but most likely an Arch hanging out for my protection.

Photo: On April 28th, 2020 this very mysterious cloud appeared above our home near Prescott Valley, Arizona.

Photo: On April 28th, 2020 another very mysterious cloud appeared above our home near Prescott Valley, Arizona.

Photo: On April 28th, 2020 this very mysterious cloud appeared above our home near Prescott Valley, Arizona. You can definitely see a face in the bottom center of the frame.

Photo: On April 28th, 2020 this very mysterious cloud appeared above our home near Prescott Valley, Arizona. You can definitely see a face in the bottom center of the frame.

Photo: An enormous storm described as an "inland hurricane" spawned tornado like winds and hail from central Texas to Wisconsin and left behind this very mysterious orange cloud formation in Oklahoma after a tornado touch down on April 28th, 2020.

Photo: The morning of April 30th, 2020 this amazing sunrise appeared on my way to do a morning rosary at Sacred Heart Catholic Church in Prescott, Arizona after the eruption of a volcano in Russia that sparked "apocalyptic fears" after covering an entire city in ash.

Photo: The evening of April 30th, 2020 this amazingly beautiful sunset appeared directly above our home in Prescott Valley, Arizona after a morning rosary asking St. Mary for more "signs in the skies" and for this world to disarm and turn away from war and greed.

Photo: Apocalyptic "spider lightning" lights up the skies on April 30th, 2020 in Oklahoma.

Photo: Another amazing glimpse of the sunset near our home in Prescott Valley, Arizona on April 30th, 2020 as taken by my wife Carol Rose Kloss (The "New Rose").

On May 2nd, 2020 a flurry of earthquakes struck: a 4.6 magnitude and 5.4 magnitude hit Puerto Rico, and a 5.4 magnitude and 6.6 magnitude hit Greece. On May 3rd, 2020 a magnitude 3.3 earthquake struck Los Angeles as a 5.9 magnitude earthquake struck Japan as the Sakurajima volcano erupted strongly.

On May 3rd, 2020 a very powerful storm drenched Arkansas with torrential rains as strong winds knocked out power for 130,000 in Tennessee. On May 4th, 2020 a 5.6 magnitude earthquake struck near Japan as an asteroid the size of a bus flew 4,350 miles above the Pacific Ocean making it the closest pass of an asteroid near earth on record.

Photo: An amazing view of the new sun while hiking near Lake Powell, Arizona on May 2nd, 2020. Notice the green orb present again in mid frame.

Photo: A dangerous apocalyptic "derecho" storm hits Nashville, Tennessee on May 5th, 2020 causing major power outages with 70 m.p.h. winds.

Photo: A major storm front in South Carolina on May 5th, 2020 bringing major lightning strikes.

On May 6th, 2020, a massive 6.9 magnitude earthquake struck Indonesia as a massive dust storm engulfed the capital city of Niger, turning the sky red and terrifying residents. Also, on May 6th, 2020 near Seattle, an exploding meteor created a sonic boom and lit up the sky as it "rattled bones" of local residents. On May 7th, 2020, a 6.1 magnitude earthquake struck near Papua New Guinea, and the Sernageomin volcano in Chile erupted, sending ash over 18,000 feet into the air. Also, on May 7th, 2020, a 5.1 magnitude earthquake struck Iran, causing casualties. On May 8th, 2020 headlines read "Mother's Day weekend could bring bomb cyclone, thundersnow to northeast." On May 9th, 2020, a 5.3 magnitude earthquake struck the Philippines.

On May 10th, 2020, a 5.5 magnitude earthquake struck Chile, as a 4.5 magnitude earthquake rattled residents near San Diego, CA, a 5.6 magnitude earthquake hit Indonesia, and a 5.8 magnitude earthquake hit Japan. Also on May 10th, 2020, powerful storms hit central Ohio, leaving thousands without power, and bringing down wires and trees as the Sakurajima volcano in Japan erupted strongly on May 8th, 9th, and 10th. Also on May 10th, 2020, a large meteor flew across the sky near Baton Rouge, Louisiana, creating a fireball. On May 11th, 2020, a morning earthquake hit Rome, as another earthquake hit northern Israel, and an earthquake hit Pyongyang in North Korea. All three quakes were in the 3.3-3.8 magnitude range. On May 12th, 2020, a 6.6 magnitude earthquake struck near Vanuatu in the South Pacific. On May 13th, 2020, a magnitude 5.7 earthquake struck Chile.

On May 14th, 2020, an inbound meteor created a fireball along the southeastern coast of the United States. On May 15th, 2020, a magnitude 4.9 earthquake and a much larger 6.5 magnitude earthquake struck Nevada, and a magnitude earthquake struck Samoa. Also, on May 15th, 2020 headlines read that the first hurricane named Arthur is starting to form in the Atlantic, as parts of Texas and Oklahoma may see severe storms and flooding. On May 16th, 2020, a magnitude earthquake struck Alberta, Canada, and a 5.3 magnitude earthquake struck Samoa. On May 17th, 2020, a magnitude 5.4 earthquake struck near Fiji.

On May 18th, 2020, a 5.5 magnitude earthquake struck off the coast of Eureka, CA, a 5.3 magnitude earthquake struck Japan, and a 5.8 magnitude earthquake struck 62 miles from Greece. Also, on May 18th, 2020, Category 5 Cyclone Amphion, the most powerful storm ever recorded in the Bay of Bengal, started making its way toward the northeastern coast of India, as tropical storm Arthur took aim at the coastline of North Carolina. On May 19th, 2020 a fireball meteor exploded over England, disturbing wildlife in an amazing display. On May 20th, 2020, my former hometown of Midland, Michigan saw major flooding that threatened to leave the city under nine feet of water. Rare May snowstorms hit the Sierra Nevada mountains of California, and a 5.0 magnitude earthquake struck Tonopah, Nevada. Also, on May 20th, 2020, the Amancaya volcano in Peru erupted strongly, sending ash 24,000 feet into the air, and a 6.2 magnitude earthquake struck in the Mediterranean.

On May 21st, 2020 news headlines read, "NASA scientists claim to have discovered evidence of a parallel universe where time moves backwards." The article discussed a cosmic ray detection experiment that found particles outside our universe that may actually be moving backwards in time. This indicates there is a parallel universe where the rules of the standard model of physics do not apply. This certainly would fit with my spiritual experiences of being visited by passed on spirits who no longer seem to be confined to one time/space dimension, as well as suggests the existence of "the other kingdom of Heaven" which is eternal and never ending. This new scientific finding would certainly fit with the images of "infinity" displayed in this book.

Photo: The morning of May 6th, 2020 his amazing sunrise appeared over the mountains near our home in Prescott Valley, Arizona while on my way for a morning rosary at Sacred Heart Catholic Church in Prescott, Arizona. It appears to me as an angel in flight. As I pulled into the church Annunaki Angel half-breed Sarah MacLachlan's song "Angel" came on the radio. I can't think of a better way to start my day.

Photo: A very oddly shaped cloud that appears to me as a beast in flight with wings, four legs, head and tail and is very similar to William Blake's interpretation of the Great Red Dragon. This cloud appeared the evening of May 6th, 2020 after a morning rosary asking St. Mary and all the angels and saints to bind Lucifer/Hillel Ben Shachar/Memnoch/Satan/red dragon/devil and all of his lions of the night from being able to host any man, woman, or child.

Photo: The third and final "supermoon" the evening of May 6th, 2020. Notice the very large blue-green object in the top of the frame. I have captured similar objects in other photos of the sun that I have enclosed in previous volumes of The New Wine, but this is the first time I have ever photographed the moon with such a mysterious orb present in the frame.

Photo: A meteor explodes over the Pacific Northwest creating a loud sonic boom and rattling local residents' bones on May 6th, 2020.

Photo: On May 7th, 2020 this very mysterious face appeared in the skies above our home near Prescott Valley, Arizona.

Photo: An amazing view of the final super blood moon the night of May 7th, 2020. The moon appeared very red and almost looked like the sun setting above the Mingus Mountains of Prescott Valley, Arizona.

Photo: On May 8th, 2020 a very mysterious figure appeared in the clouds above our home near Prescott Valley, Arizona.

Photo: On May 9th, 2020 after two full rosaries at Sacred Heart Catholic Church in Prescott, Arizona in which I prayed for world peace, for the world to turn away from greed, and for those responsible for the release of COVID-19 to be held responsible and to be wrapped in St. Michael's wings the above image appeared in the skies directly above our home in Prescott Valley, Arizona. To me there is no doubt this is St. Michael's wing.

Photo: Another angel cloud wing from May 9th, 2020 above our home in Prescott Valley, Arizona.

Photo: Another amazing cloud formation on May 9th, 2020 the day before a bomb cyclone was set to hit the northeast bringing May snow showers. I clearly see a demonic looking face in the bottom center of the frame.

Photo: Sunrise the morning of May 10th, 2020 (Mother's Day) near Prescott Valley, Arizona while on the way to recite two full rosaries at Sacred Heart Catholic Church in Prescott, Arizona for world peace and for the world to turn away from idolatry and greed.

Photo: A new painting I completed on May 10th, 2020 (Mother's Day) which I call "The Eagle." I painted this amazing symbol of American freedom a day after the Vatican released a lengthy statement regarding the COVID-19 coronavirus which governments are using to infringe upon people's God given rights and initiate tracking systems meant to monitor private citizens.

Photo: The sunrise the morning of May 11th, 2020 near Sacred Heart Catholic Church in Prescott, Arizona to recite a full rosary for world peace and for the world to turn away from greed. Notice how two mysterious orbs are now present.

Photo: The sunset near Prescott Valley, Arizona on May 11th, 2020. Notice the green orb present again surrounded by a red ring. The sun was dancing and shimmering as it disappeared to the west.

Photo: The amazing sunrise the morning of May 14th, 2020 in Tucson, Arizona while on my way to work with local retina surgeons assisting with visualization for complex eye surgeries.

Photo: On May 16th, 2020 after hiking with my wife Carol Rose in Sedona, this amazing cloud image appeared directly above our home in Prescott Valley, Arizona. What is amazing about this image was on our ride home I asked St. Mary if she could draw an "infinity eight" in the sky as a cloud. Eight is a very spiritual number and is a number associated with Christ and infinity.

Photo: I have outlined the "infinity eight" as a cloud (with the image now rotated ninety degrees to show the number eight) that appeared directly above our home in Prescott Valley, Arizona on May 16th, 2020 after hiking with my wife Carol Rose in the spiritually uplifting community of Sedona, Arizona.

On the drive home, I asked St. Mary if she could draw me an "infinity eight" in the sky as a cloud. It appears she definitely delivered.

As you may recall, if you read the first volume of The New Wine right before young Paxton Nathaniel Elkins died at the age of 8 from diffuse intrinsic pontine glioma, we asked him at the church we prayed with him at in Valparaiso, Indiana if he had anything he wanted to say to Mary and Jesus, and he said without hesitation, "yes, tell them I love them more than the numbers that never stop."

Here was a dying boy demonstrating knowledge of both "other kingdom keys" and equating the human emotion of love to mathematical infinity.

Photo: Shortly after the "infinity figure eight" cloud appeared above our home in Prescott Valley, Arizona on May 16th, 2020 this amazing angel wing cloud formed nearby in the sky.

Photo: An incredibly beautiful sunset the night of May 16th, 2020 near Prescott Valley, Arizona after a day filled with amazing signs and wonders in the sky.

Photo: The first Son Jesus Christ as a statue outside Sacred Heart Catholic Church near Prescott, Arizona the morning of May 17th, 2020 before a rosary and morning mass. If you look above the church you can see an amazing angel hovering within a cloud. I will show a blow up of the same image below.

Photo: The hovering angel within the cloud above Sacred Heart Catholic Church near Prescott, Arizona the morning of May 17th, 2020 before a rosary and morning mass. I decided to name this particular angel "Roger" after the former Roman Catholic Priest who married my wife and I and who is currently battling terminal cancer very courageously.

Photo: An amazing sunset the night of May 17th, 2020 over the skies near Prescott Valley, Arizona.

On May 21st, 2020, a 5.3 magnitude earthquake struck near Tonopah, Nevada, and a meteor lit up the skies above Spokane, Washington. On May 22nd, 2020, a magnitude 6.1 earthquake struck off the west coast of Mexico as Mt. Etna in Italy erupted, sending ash into the air.

On May 23rd, 2020, a magnitude 5.2 earthquake hit Chile. Also, on May 23rd, 2020 headlines read, "two left dead in the Carolinas as tens of thousands without power" after strong storms hit the east coast, and severe storms in Illinois threatened the safety of 40 million Americans.

Also, on May 23rd, 2020 a 5.6 magnitude earthquake struck near Mauritius, a 5.9 magnitude earthquake struck near South Africa, a 5.5 magnitude earthquake struck near Mexico, and a 5.1 magnitude earthquake caused injuries in Iran.

On May 24th, 2020, a strong 5.8 magnitude earthquake struck New Zealand. Also on May 24th, headlines read, "once in a decade, a storm leaves 50,000 without power and triggers dust storms in Australia." The article mentioned that winds of over 72 m.p.h. battered the west coast of Australia, causing power outages.

On May 25th, 2020, a 5.4 magnitude earthquake struck near Guam, the Karymsky volcano in Russia erupted ash 17,000 feet into the air as softball sized hail pounded central Texas, tornadoes touched down in Illinois, and a 5.1 magnitude earthquake struck India.

On May 26th, 2020, a 5.4 magnitude earthquake struck near Vanuatu, and on May 27th, 2020, a stronger 6.4 magnitude earthquake struck near Vanuatu.

On May 27th, 2020 headlines read, "tropical storm Bertha makes landfall in South Carolina" and more "severe storms possible across central Texas."

On May 28th, 2020, a huge fireball exploded in the sky above Turkey as a meteor streaked across the sky. Also, on May 28th, 2020, a 5.8 and 5.9 magnitude earthquake struck near Tonga.

On May 29th, 2020, a powerful 5.2 magnitude earthquake struck near Nagano, Japan, and a 4.7 magnitude earthquake rattled New Delhi, India, shaking buildings as a 5.5 magnitude earthquake struck in the South Pacific.

On May 30th, 2020, a 5.5 magnitude earthquake struck Indonesia and a 5.6 magnitude earthquake struck near the coast of Japan as a strong 6.1 magnitude earthquake struck Peru.

On May 31st, 2020 headlines read, "for the first time in history, a third tropical storm formed prior to hurricane season, as tropical storm Amanda leaves destructive flooding in El Salvador and Guatemala."

Recent headlines also read, "researchers predict up to 19 named storms during this hurricane season of 2020." On June 2nd, 2020 headlines read "Cristobal becomes earliest third Atlantic storm on record."

On June 3rd, 2020, a 5.7 magnitude earthquake hit Indonesia as a 5.9 magnitude earthquake struck Tonga, and a large 6.8 magnitude earthquake struck Chile as a 5.5 magnitude earthquake rattled homes in Los Angeles, CA. Also, on June 3rd, 2020 headlines read an asteroid the size of the Empire State Building set to pass safely past Earth.

On June 4th, 2020, a strong 6.4 magnitude earthquake struck near Indonesia.

Photo: The afternoon of May 22nd, 2020 in the skies above our home near Prescott Valley, Arizona this amazing image of an angel in the clouds appeared while walking my dogs. What is very fascinating to me about this angel appearing is it came on the heels of a tragic accident in which Captain Jennifer Casey of the Canadian Snowbirds lost her life in a tragic airplane accident while training for an event meant to boost spirits in Canada during the difficult time of this pandemic. Seeing photos of Jen Casey online makes me believe she is definitely one of my Mother Mary's angel "half-breeds" and it is quite likely this is her now showing what she can do in her new life.

Photo: Canadian Snowbirds Captain Jenn Casey (with the initials J.C.) who tragically died after a mishap with her plane crashing while practicing to perform a show in hopes of lifting the spirits of Canadians during this global pandemic. I believe it is highly likely that the image of the angel that appeared to me on May 22nd, 2020 is Angel Jenn Casey saying hello to us all. Captain Casey loved what she was doing for a living and was known as a gifted storyteller among family and friends. She will now be looking over us all from her lofty perch on high as she has been granted a new set of wings.

Photo: An amazing sunset the evening of May 22nd, 2020 near our home in Prescott Valley, Arizona. This sunset came after record setting supercell storms formed over Texas.

Photo: On May 22nd, 2020 this amazing supercell storm formed in Texas creating some of the most powerful winds on record as it rotated more than sixty thousand feet in the air. This is an incredible display of God The Father's awesome power. I believe these types of apocalyptic events will continue until this world disarms it weapons and turns away from war and greed.

Photo: An incredibly mysterious cloud formation above our home in Prescott Valley, Arizona on May 23rd, 2020 after a morning rosary. There is definitely a powerful presence in the middle of this cloud and the energy it gave off was quite remarkable. If you look closely you can see a mysterious face in the middle of the cloud.

Photo: The morning of May 23rd, 2020 while reciting a morning rosary at Sacred Heart Catholic Church in Prescott, Arizona I asked St. Mary if she could show us Our Father's Hand in the sky. The above photo appeared exactly at 3 p.m. I can see a large hand in the middle of the frame.

Photo: In case you didn't see the hand in the previous photo I have outlined it in blue above. This amazing sign showed up at exactly 3p.m. on May 23rd, 2020 after a morning rosary where I asked St. Mary to show Our Father's Hand in the sky as a sign, he is directing the apocalypse. When I showed these images to a friend, they saw a dove which is also a symbol of peace and the Father's Holy Spirit.

Photo: Shortly after Our Father's Hand appeared in the skies above Prescott Valley, Arizona on May 23rd, 2020 the clouds turned into one large angel wing covering the entire sky.

Photo: A second view of the entire sky as an angel wing on May 23rd, 2020 near our home in Prescott Valley, Arizona.

Photo: An incredibly mysterious cloud formation in the skies above Prescott Valley, Arizona on May 24th, 2020. I see the face of a lion to the middle right of the frame

Photo: An amazing image which appears to be a face in the middle left of the sky as well as another face to the bottom right of the frame above our home near Prescott Valley, Arizona on May 24th, 2020.

Photo: Another angel in flight in the skies above Prescott Valley, Arizona on May 24th, 2020.

Photo: An amazing image of assembling angels in the sky on May 24th, 2020 above our home near Prescott Valley, Arizona.

Photo: This incredible view of the "other kingdom" which is a "sundome" came at exactly 2 p.m. on May 27th, 2020 after three full rosaries at Sacred Heart Catholic Church in Prescott, Arizona. This image is stunning beyond words, multiple orbs, halos and rays from Heaven/Eden/An.

Photo: On May 30th, 2020 after a morning rosary at St. Germaine Catholic Church in Prescott Valley, Arizona this incredible image of an angel hovering with wings behind his back and head bowed in prayer appeared in the skies.

This angel appeared exactly three hours after I completed my rosary, and later I was informed by a relative that there was a worldwide rosary at exactly that time, as well unbeknownst to me at the time. Pope Francis presided over the rosary, and comes on the eve of Pentecost, and was dedicated to Our Lady of Fatima (St. Mary).

On the same day the angel appeared in our skies on May 30th, 2020, my sister Katherine sent me an amazing photo of her daughter named Priya. Priya's father is Indian, and the translation of her name means "Beloved." We knew very early that Priya was a very special child, as she started calling my mother, her grandmother Barbara Pinard, the name "Yawa", which is very close phonetically to Yahweh. The image below was not Photoshop in anyway.

It clear shows half a rainbow halo tracing the right side of her body in the photo, and is similar to the paintings of St. Mary as the Virgin of Guadalupe, showing a similar rainbow halo surrounding her when she appears as an apparition to deliver a message.

Photo: A half rainbow halo in May 2020 surrounding my niece Priya who is three years old and a very spiritual and special child.

Photo: An amazing artist illustration of the Virgin of Guadalupe (St. Mary) surrounded by a similar rainbow halo as she appears to deliver an important message from Heaven/Eden/An.

Photo: On the evening of May 30th, 2020 while the song "Roadhouse Blues" by The Doors came on the radio this sunset appeared above Prescott Valley, Arizona. This song is a particular favorite of mine as it refers directly to St. Mary with the lyrics "Ashen lady, give up your vows, save our city, right now."

Photo: The sunset above Prescott Valley, Arizona on May 30th, 2020 quickly morphed into this amazing image of pink laced blue clouds. It is one of the most amazing images I've ever seen in nature and shortly after one of my Mother Mary's favorite Doors song came on the radio.

Photo: One of the most incredibly beautiful sunsets I've ever seen the evening of May 31st, 2020 near our home in Prescott Valley, Arizona in yet another glimpse of the other kingdom of Heaven/Eden/An.

Photo: Another amazing one-of-a-kind sunset the evening of June 1st, 2020 near Prescott Valley, Arizona. I showed this photo to my cousin Carly who has a Master's Degree in Divinity and she sees a flaming sword at the top of the frame which is very symbolic of the times we are currently in of major spiritual combat.

Photo: A close up of the flaming sword from my photo of the sunset on June 1st, 2020, I might also suggest this looks like an angel wing in flight as well, or could it possibly be another glimpse of the "Angel with a sword in his left hand" described from the vision of Lucia from her prophetic interactions with St. Mary at Fatima in 1917.

Photo: An amazing image in the skies directly above our home in Prescott Valley, Arizona on June 2nd, 2020. The amazing cloud formation appears to me as two eyes looking down and to the left of the frame. It is beautiful beyond words.

Photo: On June 3rd, 2020 one day after the mysterious "eyes" appeared in the clouds in our skies near Prescott Valley, Arizona this deadly and rare "derecho" swept across New Jersey with 90 m.p.h. winds killing four people.

Photo: An incredible mysterious and angelic cloud above our home near Prescott Valley, Arizona on June 4th, 2020.

Photo: An amazing angel cloud lit with the sunset on June 4th, 2020 in the skies near our home in Prescott Valley, Arizona.

Photo: An amazing sunset the evening of June 5th, 2020 near our home in Prescott Valley, Arizona. Yet more proof of our Mother Mary's presence in our world.

On June 5th, 2020 a 5.0 magnitude earthquake struck Turkey sending people out into the streets in a panic as the Sakurajima volcano in Japan erupted again sending ash 11,000 feet into the air. Also, on June 5th, 2020 an asteroid dubbed LD2020 measuring 100 meters in diameter traveling at 60,826 m.p.h. came closer to the earth than even the moon and scientists didn't discover its pass until two days later.

On June 6th, 2020 a magnitude 5.7 earthquake struck near Fiji as another rare derecho storm brought 110 m.p.h. winds across Colorado.

On June 7th, 2020 a magnitude 5.7 earthquake struck near the Solomon Islands, a 5.9 magnitude earthquake struck near Papua New Guinea and a 5.4 magnitude earthquake struck Peru. Also, on June 7th, 2020 a meteor fireball exploded over Tennessee igniting 120 more fireball meteor sightings across 12 states and Canada.

On June 8th, 2020 a 5.6 magnitude earthquake struck Indonesia as another meteor fireball exploded along the east coast of the United States. Also, on June 8th, 2020 the Popocatepetl volcano in Mexico was rocked by 350 blasts of lava and ash in just 24 hours.

On June 9th, 2020 a magnitude 5.7 earthquake struck Iran and headlines read "an asteroid the size of six football fields will speed by earth Saturday night." Also, on June 9th, 2020 the Sangay volcano in Ecuador's Amazon region erupted leaving several cities covered in ash as a 5.9 magnitude earthquake struck near Fiji.

June 10th, 2020 saw more wildfires rage in Arizona and California as a 6.0 magnitude earthquake struck near St. Helena in the South Atlantic. Also on June 10th, 2020, deadly flooding forced the evacuation of 228,000 people in China as severe storms hit West Michigan, my former home, and left 230,000 without power after 70 m.p.h. winds and hail struck the state. Also on June 10th, 2020, another fireball meteor exploded in Europe and was witnessed by 120 observers in the UK, Germany, France, Italy and the Netherlands. On June 11th, 2020, a 5.8 magnitude earthquake struck south of South Africa.

On June 12th, 2020 headlines read "three monster asteroids headed for Earth in the month of June."

On June 13th, 2020, a strong 6.7 magnitude earthquake struck 80 miles south of Japan in the east China Sea, as a 6.0 magnitude earthquake struck near Taiwan as tropical storm Nuri headed toward the coastline of China.

On June 14th, 2020, a 5.1 magnitude earthquake struck India, as a 5.7 magnitude earthquake struck Turkey.

On June 15th, 2020, a mysterious green meteor streaked across the skies above Australia as a 5.7 magnitude earthquake struck Tajikistan. Also, on June 15th, 2020, the Fuego volcano in Guatemala and the Shiveluch volcano in Russia erupted again.

On June 16th, 2020, a 5.4 magnitude earthquake struck near the coast of Eilat in the Red Sea, as a 5.6 magnitude earthquake struck near Samoa. Also, on June 16th, 2020 headlines read "a football field sized asteroid just missed Earth and no one saw it coming." The article described a huge asteroid that passed closer to Earth than the moon's orbit, and it wasn't discovered until after it passed.

On June 18th, 2020, a massive 7.4 magnitude earthquake struck near New Zealand, creating a tsunami alert as a strong 4.2 magnitude earthquake struck Anchorage, Alaska. I found the 7.4 magnitude earthquake fascinating, because it came on the day of my sister Katherine's 41st birthday and equaled the last two numbers of my birth year of 1974.

On June 19th, 2020, a 5.6 magnitude earthquake struck near Fiji, and headlines read, "a massive asteroid the size of the Eiffel Tower in France will fly by Earth in the next few days." Also, on June 19th, 2020, a 4.9 magnitude earthquake struck central Nevada. On June 20th, 2020 news outlets reported that the Hawaiian volcano Kilauea has created nearly 20 cracks in the earth's surface as lava flows continue destructive paths after nearly seven weeks of uninterrupted eruption, spewing out 26 gallons of lava, destroying more than 500 buildings and forcing evacuations. Also, on June 20th, 2020 headlines read, "gigantic swarm of locusts hit East Africa, threatening millions with hunger," as a 5.7 magnitude earthquake struck near Iceland, and a gigantic sand storm threatened the southern United States, Mexico and the Caribbean.

On June 21st, 2020, Mt. Merapai in Indonesia erupted, sending ash over 6 kilometers into the air, as the Placaya volcano also erupted in Central America, and headlines read "asteroid three times the size of Big Ben to hurtle past Earth next week."

Also, on June 21st, 2020, a 5.8 magnitude earthquake hit India and a strong 6.0 magnitude earthquake struck near Iceland, as a 4.2 magnitude earthquake struck Oklahoma as protestors filled the streets following a President Trump re-election rally.

On June 22nd, 2020 headlines read, "over 100 million people are at risk for severe storms in the central U.S.." and a 5.5 magnitude earthquake struck near New Zealand.

On June 23rd, 2020, a massive 7.4 magnitude earthquake struck near Mexico, as a 5.9 magnitude earthquake struck in Indonesia and a second 5.9 magnitude earthquake struck near Guam.

On June 24th, 2020 headlines read, "The giant Godzilla Sahara dust storm scene from a million miles away headed towards the United States is the largest in decades." Also, on June 24th, 2020, a 6.1 magnitude earthquake struck near Bakersfield, CA and a 5.9 magnitude earthquake struck near Japan.

On June 25th, 2020 a strong 6.4 magnitude earthquake struck China. On June 26th, 2020, severe storms left over 20,000 without power and destroyed many homes in West Michigan.

On June 27th, 2020, a 4.8 magnitude earthquake struck Puerto Rico. On June 28th, 2020, a 5.5 magnitude earthquake struck near Turkey.

On June 29th, 2020, a 5.6 magnitude earthquake struck near St. Helena in the Atlantic Ocean.

On June 30th, 2020, a magnitude 5.1 earthquake struck central Nevada.

Photo: Another very rare "derecho" storm brought 110 m.p.h. winds to Colorado on June 6th, 2020.

Photo: The amazingly beautiful sunrise the morning of June 8th, 2020 after The New Wine Volume III: The Veil Rent was released internationally online over the weekend. I am praying this is a hopeful sign for the entire world to turn away from war and greed and to disarm all weapons of mass destruction immediately. Notice the bright orb surrounded by red/purple halo to the bottom right of the frame. This photo was taken on my way to say a full rosary at Sacred Heart Catholic Church in Prescott, Arizona.

Photo: An amazing sunset the evening of June 8th, 2020 near Prescott Valley, Arizona. The sun danced and shimmered brightly before setting in the west. Notice again the bright orb surrounded by red/purple halo.

Photo: Wildfires raging in the mountains north of Tucson, Arizona as seen from my hotel parking lot on June 10th, 2020 while traveling to work with local retina surgeons to assist with visualization during retina surgery. Similar fires were also raging in California. When I see these images, I think about The Doors song L.A. Woman in which Jim and I sang "I see your hair is burning, hills are filled with fire, if they say I never loved you, you know they are a liar."

Photo: An apocalyptic fire rages in the hills near Tucson, Arizona the evening of June 10th, 2020.

Photo: The beaches of Lake Michigan near my former home on June 10th, 2020 as powerful storms brought 70 m.p.h. winds and hail leaving 230,000 without power.

Photo: An amazingly beautiful sunrise near Tucson, Arizona on June 11th, 2020 on my way to work with local retina surgeons at St. Joseph's Hospital.

Photo: The evening of June 12th, 2020 this incredibly beautiful sunset appeared in the skies near our home in Prescott Valley, Arizona at the exact minute the song "Riders on the Storm" by The Doors came on Classic Vinyl on Sirius radio. The announcer stated a profound truth by saying "there's a lot of that currently going around" in reference to the number of apocalyptic storms the world has seen this year.

Photo: On the evening of June 12th, 2020 after seeing one of the most beautiful sunsets I've ever seen just as "Riders on The Storm" by The Doors came on the radio at the same moment, I soon after completed this acrylic painting of a "psychedelic deer."

"THE PARACLETE"

The Christian doctrine of the Holy Trinity (Latin: Tinitas or triad from trinus or "threefold") holds that God is one God, but three consubstantial persons or hypostases of The Father, The Son (Jesus Christ), and The Holy Spirit or "paraclete" as "one God in three Divine persons."

As I stated in previous versions of The New Wine, I believe myself to be the reincarnation of James Douglas Morrison. I have the exact same mole, same singing voice, and knew the lyrics to all Doors songs before I heard them. I also believe that it is possible to have more than one incarnation of the Son on earth simultaneously.

I personally believe that was who Paxton Nathaniel Elkins was, and I also believe Chris Cornell of the bands Soundgarden and Audioslave was also part of the "scattered sun" from the song "Waiting for the Sun" by the Doors. Many of Chris Cornell's lyrics have come true as prophecies since his passing.

Photo: On June 13th, 2020 I said a rosary at St. Germaine Catholic Church in Prescott Valley, Arizona and asked to be shown The Holy Spirit (paraclete) in the sky at exactly 3p.m. At exactly 3p.m. on a previously cloudless day this amazing image appeared directly above our home in Prescott Valley, Arizona. This image shows a panoramic view of a huge figure with a head and two enormous wings outstretched directly above our home as also seen in the images below.

Photo: Another amazing view of the Holy Spirit Angel with wings appearing directly above our home near Prescott Valley, Arizona at exactly 3p.m. on June 13th, 2020 after a rosary in the morning where I asked to see the paraclete to appear in the sky at 3p.m.

Photo: The enormous Holy Spirit (paraclete) cloud directly above our home near Prescott Valley, Arizona, the wings were so long I could not include them in this non-panoramic frame but will show them in separate frames below. When I showed the video of this appearance of the paraclete to a Roman Catholic Priest he said to me "you are gifted by God and Mary, cherish and follow."

Photo: The outstretched right wing cloud of the Holy Spirit (paraclete) image that appeared above our home at exactly 3p.m. on June 13th, 2020.

Photo: The left wing of the Holy Spirit (paraclete) image that was so long it covered most of the sky above our home near Prescott Valley, Arizona at 3p.m. on June 13th, 2020.

On the evening of June 13th, 2020, following the appearance of The Holy Spirit (paraclete) in the skies above our home, my wife watched a movie called "Mr. Brooks" about a serial killer played by actor Kevin Costner.

I found the movie dark and disturbing, and went to sleep in a guest room in our home. I woke up in the middle of the night to see what appeared to me, as my wife standing in the room with her back turned toward me.

I said out loud three times, "Carol, what are you doing in here?"

The figure then turned to me, and I could immediately see it was not my wife, but a dark demonic figure who's face turned black the second I saw it face to face. I immediately jumped out of bed and went down our hallway to find my wife standing in front of her bathroom mirror moving in the same manner as the entity with its back turned toward me was moving.

In my opinion, this was definitely a trick of Hillel Ben Shachar/ Lucifer/Satan/Red Dragon/devil/Memnoch, which was a message of intimidation and fear for calling the Holy Spirit (paraclete) down to earth for protection.

When I think of this incident, the lyrics from "The Devil went down to Georgia" by Charlie Daniel's band come to mind with "the devils in the house of the rising sun."

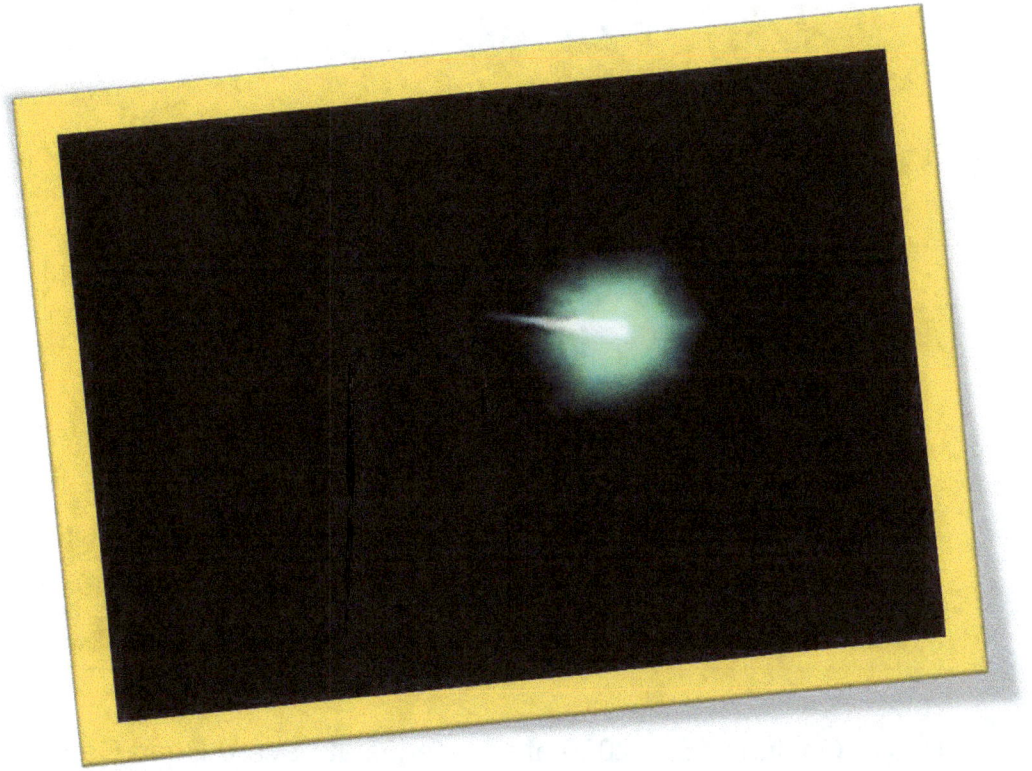

Photo: On June 15th, 2020 a mysterious green meteor streaked through the skies above Australia leaving many spectators amazed.

Photo: On June 15th, 2020 after rosaries at Sacred Heart Catholic Church and St. Germaine Catholic Church I asked St. Mary for a "bruised purple sunset" in honor of the Prophet Chris Cornell's lyrics from the song "Like A Stone" in which he sings "the sky was bruised, the wine was bled, and there you led me on." At exactly 7:30 p.m. just as "Break On Through" by The Doors played on Classic Vinyl on Sirius satellite radio the sky turned into this purple bruised sunset before setting. It appears yet another Chris Cornell prophecy has come to fruition.

"INSANITY'S HORSE ADORNS THE SKY"

One of the most prophetic songs ever written by The Doors was the song "I can't see your face in my mind." I will post some of the lyrics here and explain how this predicts the horsemen of the apocalypse:

> I Can't See Your Face in My Mind:
> I can't see your face in my mind
> I can't see your face in my mind
> Carnival dogs consume the lines
> Can't see your face in my mind
> Don't you cry
> Baby, please don't cry
> And don't look at me with your eyes
> I can't seem to find the right lie
> I can't seem to find the right lie
> Insanity's horse Adorns the sky
> Can't seem to find the right lie

Photo: On the morning of June 16th, 2020, this incredible image appeared directly above Sacred Heart Catholic Church in Prescott, Arizona, as I was reciting a rosary for world peace.

I definitely see what appears to be a "horse head" in the sky, which I found interesting because I had been contemplating a new painting of a horse. The other amazing thing that is interesting about this appearance is a line from The Doors' song "I can't see your face in my mind" in which Jim Morrison sings "insanity's horse adorns the sky."

Insanity's horse is a reference to the global pandemic in 2020, which saw thousands of deaths and modification of daily life that seems insane to many. This amazing song was also a prophecy in which Jim knew he would be with me in 2020, as these amazing signs and wonders of the apocalypse would appear, but that he couldn't back then quite "see my face in his mind" but did see a "horse adorn the sky."

Could this appearance of a horse head in the clouds signal the arrival of one of the four horsemen of the apocalypse?

Photo: On June 16th, 2020 the Bush Fire north of Phoenix, Arizona surged overnight and is quickly becoming the largest wildfire in Arizona history.

Photo: On June 19th, 2020 after a rosary at Sacred Heart Catholic Church in Prescott, Arizona this amazing image appeared in the skies directly above the church. It is simply one of the most beautiful displays of nature I have ever seen and more evidence of the other kingdom and angels on high.

Photo: An amazing image of a red angel in flight above my co-worker Kristina's family home in Spain on June 20th, 2020. Kristina was first introduced in the third volume of The New Wine: The Veil Rent and has an amazing birth story. She was born in Russia on a day when all water, including water in the womb is considered holy water. A strange woman came into her mother's hospital room and said to her "you must name this child Kristina" before disappearing.

Photo: An amazing sunset the evening of June 20th, 2020 near our home in Prescott Valley, Arizona.

Photo: On June 20th, 2020 I completed this acrylic painting that includes the angel photographed over Spain on the same day.

Photo: The "Garden of Stone" outside St. Germaine Catholic Church in Prescott Valley, Arizona during a rosary on June 21st, 2020. I believe this is a prophesy from the song "Garden" written and performed by the Prophet Eddie Vedder, lead singer of one of my favorite bands, Pearl Jam.

After the release of the first volume of The New Wine, I heard Ed say on the Pearl Jam Sirius radio channel, "I'm not Jesus in the band, but I look like him."

Yes, I heard you Ed, and yes, you are me too, and you have kingship and are part of the "scattered sun" as well from the prophetic song "Waiting for the Sun" by The Doors.

It is in this location that saying a full rosary for world peace led to the image of the angel hovering in the sky, bowing its head, and the appearance of the Holy Spirit (paraclete) above my home. This is definitely a very spiritually powerful garden of stone.

Photo: An amazing sunset the evening of June 21st, 2020 near our home in Prescott Valley, Arizona.

Photo: The very rare "ring of fire" solar eclipse as seen from India on June 21st, 2020. Many spiritualists see these ring of fire solar eclipses as preludes to immense inner spiritual growth. In fact, many foreign nations include his image on their country's flags.

Photo: An incredible image taken directly above our home near Prescott Valley, Arizona on June 21st, 2020. I see what appears to be a demonic looking figure in flight with its right arm bending and reaching towards its center. This came after a day of three full rosaries at local churches asking for our other kingdom Anunnaki Angels to drive demons and lions of the night out of mankind and off of the earth.

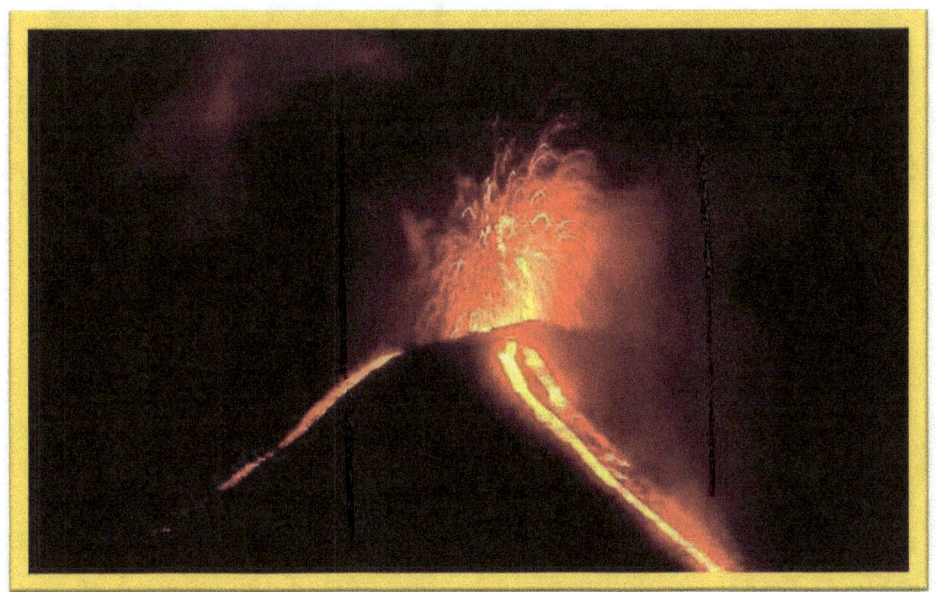

Photo: On June 21st, 2020 the Pacaya volcano in Central America erupted sending lava streaming down the mountain. In my daily prayers I say to St. Mary "bring earthquake, volcano, hurricane, cyclone, derecho, tornado, meteor, asteroid, tsunami, wildfire and flood until this world accepts our two keys, until this world disarms, and until this world turns from war and greed."

Photo: An amazingly beautiful sunset the evening of June 23rd, 2020 near Prescott Valley, Arizona on a day that saw a powerful 7.4 magnitude earthquake strike southern Mexico killing seven people and shaking building hundreds of miles away in Mexico City.

Photo: This incredible image shows an angel in flight, wings spread, chest forward as it appeared directly above Sacred Heart Catholic Church the morning of June 24th, 2020 after a full rosary for world peace, and for the world to disarm all weapons of mass destruction and turn away from greed. I would not uncover the significance of this angel's appearance until one day later which I will explain below.

Photo: This is an undated photo of Matthew Joseph Barr born October 15th, 1979 with his mother Lori Martello. Lori is a very skilled and kind surgical technologist that I work with during retina surgery at St. Joseph's Hospital in Tucson, Arizona. Lori is known for her world-famous jams. Sadly, Matthew passed away unexpectedly on Sunday, June 21st, 2020 (Father's Day) exactly three days prior to the angel appearing above Sacred Heart Catholic Church in Prescott, Arizona as shown above on June 24th, 2020. Both Lori and I believe this is Matthew, now an angel, showing off his new flight skills above Arizona.

Photo: This amazing "fish" cloud appeared directly above downtown Prescott, Arizona on June 24th, 2020 after a morning rosary for world peace and for the world to turn away from greed. The odd coincidence is I had just watched the movie "Big Fish" starring Anunnaki Angel half breeds Billy Crudup and Marion Cotillard. The movie has many spiritual teachings in it about human nature.

Photo: An enormous apocalyptic "Godzilla" Saharan dust storm as photographed from space making its way across the Atlantic Ocean in late June 2020 is the largest in decades and will cover the Caribbean and southern United States.

Photo: An amazing image of one of my father's Arch Angel's right wing (most likely St. Michael if I had to guess) as I drove home from Tucson on June 25th, 2020 after working with local retina surgeons at St. Joseph Hospital. With the state of Arizona literally on fire and huge surges in coronavirus cases this was a welcomed and comforting sight.

Photo: The large left wing of Arch Angel St. Michael that appeared directly across the other side of the freeway near Tucson, Arizona on June 25th, 2020 after working with local retina surgeons. You can see how vast his reach is across the sky.

Photo: The morning of June 26th, 2020 after a full rosary at Sacred Heart Catholic Church in Prescott, Arizona this angel in flight appeared in the skies directly above the church.

Photo: On June 26th, 2020 the day of my brother Paul's 48th birthday, these large angel wings appeared directly above the roof of our home in Prescott Valley, Arizona at exactly noon PST after a morning rosary for protection, healing, world peace and for the world to turn away from greed and disarm all WMDs.

Photo: On June 26th, 2020 a few minutes after the two large wings appeared above the roof of our home in Prescott Valley, Arizona this enormous wing appeared on the opposite side of our home. It is beautiful beyond words.

Photo: On Sunday, June 28th, 2020 at exactly 3 p.m. these amazing angel wings appeared directly above the new church building at St. Germaine Catholic Church in Prescott Valley, Arizona. What happened shortly after as I was praying a rosary was simply amazing.

Photo: At exactly 3 p.m. at the "Garden of Stone" at St. Germaine Catholic Church a second pair of angel wings appeared as I said a rosary for world peace and for the world to turn away from greed. Notice also the blue/green orb/halo in the bottom middle of the frame.

Photo: Directly to the left of the angel wings above St. Germaine Catholic Church on June 28th, 2020 at exactly 3 p.m. this demonic looking face appeared, notice the large eyes and pointed ears in the middle of the frame. I also see a second demonic looking face behind it to the left.

Photo: Shortly after the first demonic looking face appeared in the skies above St. Germaine Catholic Church on June 28th, 2020 at 3 p.m. this "triple headed demon" appeared in the sky as I said a full rosary for world peace and for the world to turn away from greed.

Photo: The evening of June 28th, 2020 brought an amazingly beautiful sunset that also showed more demonic spirits being exorcised from the earth. The following photos are beyond anything I've ever encountered.

Photo: As the sun was setting on June 28th, 2020 this cloud began to take on an ominous form as something started to drop down from the middle of the cloud almost like a tornado and soon formed something quite terrifying.

Photo: The "head" of this dropping cloud then began to form on June 28th, 2020 in what appears to me as the head of a dragon or serpent before it transformed yet again into the face captured in the next frame.

Photo: The evening of June 28th, 2020 saw a dropping cloud forming this demonic looking face with horns, pointed chin, and dark orbits near the eyes. There is no doubt this is the devil or baphomet who goes by many names to include Lucifer/Hillel Ben Shachar/Memnoch/Satan/red dragon/devil or baphomet.

Photo: Another depiction of the Great Red Dragon as painted by William Blake. This depiction shows the beasts with seven horns. I am enclosing this painting because this painting looks oddly similar to the depiction of Lucifer/ Hillel Ben Shachar/Memnoch/Satan/red dragon/devil as shown above.

Photo: Another demonic looking face appeared in the clouds next to the one above in the skies near Prescott Valley, Arizona on June 28th, 2020 at sunset.

When I see such images of demonic faces in our sky it reminds me of Ephesians 6:12 which states:

"For our struggle is not against flesh and blood, but against rulers, against the authorities, against the powers of this dark world and against the spiritual forces of evil in the heavenly realms."

"THE MARK OF THE BEAST"

Spiritual forces of evil can exist in the heavenly realms. This is a paradox. Some confuse this statement with some type of collusion or cooperation between angel and demon. Nothing could be further from the truth. While each is oftentimes tempting the other to "defect" and join the other side, there is a constant struggle in our skies that permeates our thoughts, hearts, and minds, a constant balance between good and evil, light and dark that is eternal.

When I think of what is going on right at this moment in 2020, with one elite ruling class of men whose net worth exceeds hundreds of billions of dollars advocating for a world "vaccine" due to the outbreak of COVID-19, the passage from Revelations 13:16-18 immediately comes to mind that reveals unto us the identity of the Anti-Christ:

"And he causeth all, both small and great, rich and poor, free and bond, to receive a mark on their right hand, or in their foreheads:

And that no man might buy or sell, save he that had the mark, or the name of the beast, or the number of his name.

Here is wisdom. Let him that hath understanding count the number of the beast: for it is the number of a man, and his number is six hundred threescores and six."

This highly prophetic passage written centuries ago reveals the identity of the Anti-Christ and a new world order agenda used to track private citizens through the administration of a vaccine forced upon the world in response to a pandemic. This passage explains how, unless you have this mark on your hand and forehead (of being vaccinated and microchipped) you will not be able to participate in buying or selling anything (think now of required social distancing in restaurants and supermarkets) and thus becoming economically paralyzed. There is also a tie-in to the number 666, and this number is associated with the "mark of the beast."

Many online theories have stated that the current patent request of Bill Gates for his Microsoft "crypto-mining system" which converts physical or mental activity into computer power is numbered WO/2020/060606 (666). To further bolster the validity of this, the Catholic Church recently put out a very lengthy and detailed statement reinforcing that this current pandemic is indeed part of a New World Order agenda to enforce tracking systems in human populations and violate the God-given and constitutional rights of private citizens. In this author's opinion, it is not a "coincidence" that both Tony Fauci and Bill Gates gave "warnings" as recently as a few years ago about a pending pandemic outbreak that would occur shortly.

When I think of this "mark of the beast" being something related to a "mark" on your forehead, this incredibly odd image from one of my hospital visits for my job struck me as quite profound. Below is the photo from a hospital I work at with retinal surgeons to help give them visualization during retina surgery. As you walk into the hospital, you cannot gain entry until the screen you for a fever, which may be due to a coronavirus infection. They do this by placing a thermometer on your forehead.

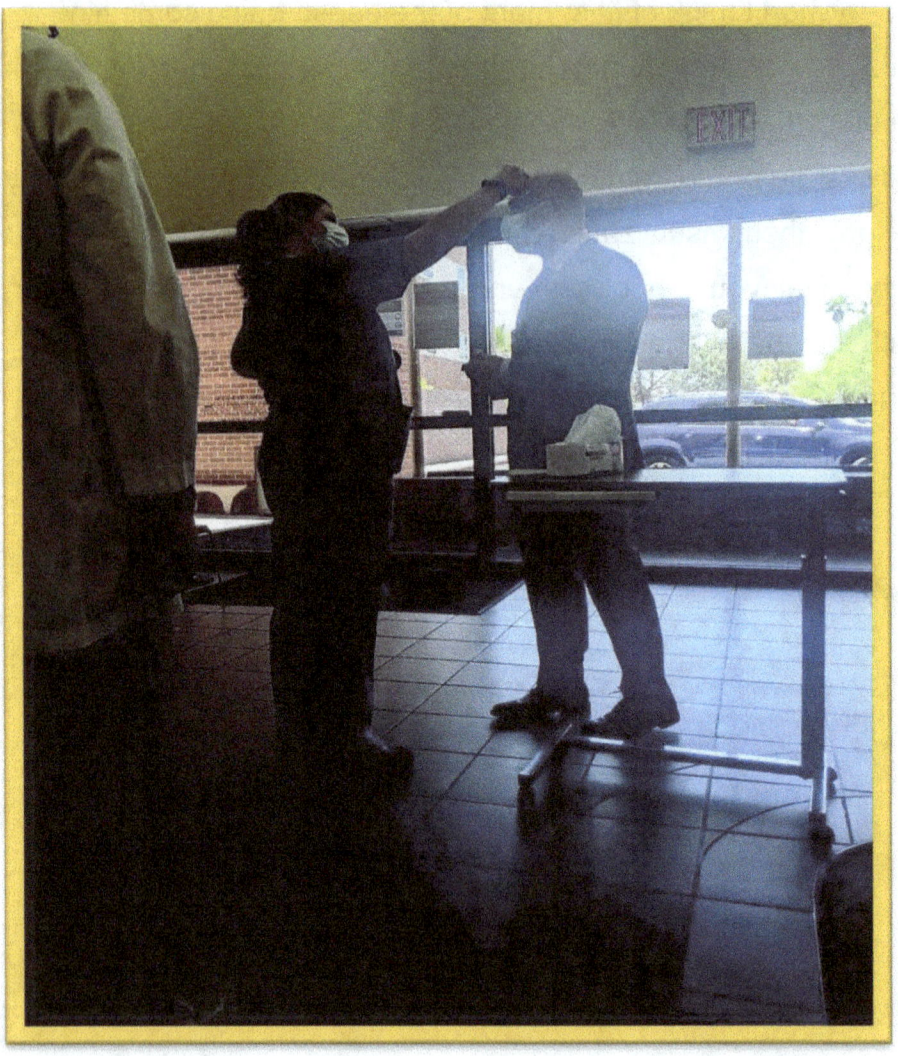

Photo: An entry screening at a local hospital in Tucson, Arizona in the summer of 2020 where I frequently work with retina surgeons to help give them visualization of the retina while they operate. Is this image here showing the "mark of the beast" as a "reading" of your body temperature by placing an electronic thermometer on your forehead? This image does seem to coincide with the current situation of the entire world being caught in a deadly pandemic that seems to be straight out of the Book of Revelations.

Photo: An incredible image in the skies above Prescott Valley, Arizona on June 29th, 2020 after a daily rosary at exactly 3 p.m. at St. Germaine Catholic Church. During my rosary I asked if I could see another angel in the sky. If you look closely enough you can see a baby faced figure with two wings lying down with what also appears to be a small animal shaped like a sea otter or weasel on its lap.

Photo: Another amazing image of animal like cloud figures floating in the skies above Prescott Valley, Arizona on June 29th, 2020 after a rosary at nearby St. Germaine Catholic Church. If you look closely the middle animal shaped figure appears to be holding a full glass of wine.

Photo: On June 29th, 2020 after a day in which I asked my Garden of Stone at St. Germaine Catholic Church to see more angels in the sky at sunset this angel wing appeared as a cloud directly above Prescott Valley, Arizona.

Photo: A second sunset lit angel cloud wing appeared above Prescott Valley, Arizona on June 29th, 2020 after a rosary at St. Germaine Catholic Church asking to see more angels in the sky directly at sunset.

On July 1st, 2020, a 5.1 magnitude earthquake struck near Vanuatu. On July 2nd, 2020, a 5.2 magnitude earthquake struck Japan as a bright meteor exploded above its skies and the Suwanosejima volcano exploded. Also, on July 2nd, 2020, a 5.1 magnitude earthquake struck Chile as a 5.2 magnitude earthquake struck Mexico.

On July 3rd, 2020, a 5.2 magnitude earthquake struck Chile as a 4.9 magnitude earthquake, and a 5.3 magnitude earthquake struck Puerto Rico, and a 4.6 magnitude earthquake struck Hawaii. On July 4th, 2020, a 5.4 magnitude earthquake struck near Tajikistan.

On July 5th, 2020, a 5.5 magnitude earthquake struck Alaska as a 5.9 magnitude earthquake struck near Vanuatu. On July 6th, 2020, a 5.5 magnitude earthquake struck in the Philippine Sea, followed by a 6.2 magnitude earthquake struck in Micronesia, followed by a stronger 6.6 magnitude earthquake in Indonesia, and a 5.6 magnitude earthquake near Japan. Also, on July 6th, 2020, the Nishino-Shima volcano in Japan saw eruptions of the highest ash plumes since 2013 up to over 27,230 feet above sea level, as the earliest fifth Atlantic named tropical storm Eduoard formed over the north Atlantic Ocean.

Also, on July 6th, 2020 headlines read "Idaho started shaking March 31st, why hasn't it stopped."

On July 8th, 2020, a 5.7 magnitude earthquake struck near Australia. On July 9th, 2020, a 5.3 magnitude earthquake struck near the Maldives.

On July 10th, 2020, tropical storm Fay formed in the Atlantic Ocean, making it the 6th earliest named storm on record as it hit the eastern coast of the United States, causing major flooding.

On July 11th, 2020, a 5.3 magnitude earthquake struck Argentina, as a 5.4 magnitude earthquake struck Papua New Guinea.

On July 12th, 2020, a 5.1 magnitude earthquake struck Venezuela and a 5.1 magnitude earthquake struck China. Also, on July 12th, 2020, a 5.3 magnitude earthquake struck Nicaragua, as a 5.2 magnitude earthquake struck Micronesia.

On July 13th, 2020, a 5.2 magnitude earthquake struck New Zealand. Also, on July 13th, 2020 headlines read "asteroid 2011 ES4 at 49 meters high will pass by the Earth closer than the moon at 18,253 m.p.h."

The pass of this large asteroid will come at 44,618 miles away from the earth, which is far closer than the moon, which is 238,588 miles away.

On July 14th, 2020, a 5.2 magnitude earthquake struck near Japan, as a 5.3 magnitude earthquake struck near Fiji and a 5.7 magnitude earthquake struck near Indonesia. Also, on July 14th, 2020, a blue green meteor streaked across the skies above Florida.

On July 15th, 2020, a 5.3 magnitude earthquake struck near Alaska and a 5.8 magnitude earthquake struck near Panama.

On July 16th, 2020, a 5.9 magnitude earthquake struck near Chile, as a massive 7.0 magnitude earthquake struck Papua New

Guinea. Also, on July 16th, 2020, an asteroid bigger than the London Eye was tracked approaching close to Earth.

On July 17th, 2020, a 6.1 magnitude earthquake struck near India as a 5.3 magnitude earthquake struck Myanmar as a 5.8 magnitude earthquake struck near the Solomon Islands. On July 18th, 2020 a 6.1 magnitude earthquake struck near Samoa and a 5.4 magnitude earthquake struck near Indonesia.

On July 19th, 2020 an extremely large double eruption of lava and ash blew from the Stromboli volcano in Italy and a 5.3 magnitude earthquake struck near Peru as a 5.2 magnitude earthquake struck near Argentina.

On July 21st, 2020 a 6.0 magnitude earthquake struck near Fiji as a very powerful 7.8 magnitude earthquake struck near Alaska. On July 22nd, 2020 a powerful 6.3 magnitude earthquake struck mainland China.

On July 23rd, 2020 a 5.5 magnitude earthquake struck Mexico. On July 24th, 2020 headlines read "Hurricane Douglas (I personally love the name) the strongest storm on the planet, moves toward Hawaii" as tropical storm Hanna the earliest 8th named storm in history strengthened as it headed towards the west Gulf of Mexico soon to become a hurricane. During the month of May 2020, the super caldera at Yellowstone National Park saw 300 earthquakes strike followed by another 100 earthquakes in June 2020 leading some to speculate if another super eruption is possible.

On July 25th, 2020 headlines read "China fears: scientists warn volcano extinct for 500,000 years may be recharging." Also, on July 25th, 2020 a 5.4 magnitude earthquake struck Fiji as a 6.3 magnitude earthquake struck Argentina.

On July 27th, 2020 a 4.7 magnitude earthquake struck near Hawaii and a 5.8 magnitude earthquake struck near the Philippines.

On July 28th, 2020 a very strong 6.1 magnitude aftershock struck near the Alaskan coast. Also, on July 28th, 2020 a car sized asteroid zipped past Earth at a range that rivals some satellites at a speed of 27,700 m.p.h. The asteroid wasn't even detected until July 26th, 2020.

On July 29th, 2020 a 5.6 magnitude earthquake struck Alaska as a 5.8 magnitude earthquake struck near Japan.

On July 30th, 2020 a 4.2 magnitude earthquake struck San Fernando, CA, a 5.6 magnitude earthquake struck the Philippines, and a 5.7 magnitude earthquake struck near Tonga.

Also, on July 30th, 2020 headlines read "Phoenix, Arizona breaks 86-year-old record as temperatures rise to 118 degrees," and "Hurricane Isaias batters Bahamas as storm targets entire U.S. East Coast." Recent headlines in July 2020 also read "something is brewing under Europe" after geologists make incredible discovery of new volcanic activity.

Photo: On July 2nd, 2020 this amazing sunset appeared after a day sightseeing with my mother Barbara. This is yet another amazing glimpse of the other kingdom. When my mother witnessed this particular sunset with me she relayed an amazing story from when she was driving my niece to see my sister in central, Oregon and a similar sunset appeared in the skies. As my mother turned the car which directed them away from this sunset in Oregon, my niece said, "nana, why did you turn the car we could have driven right into heaven." This is an amazing instance of a four-year-old child having intimate knowledge of the other kingdom and how to get there.

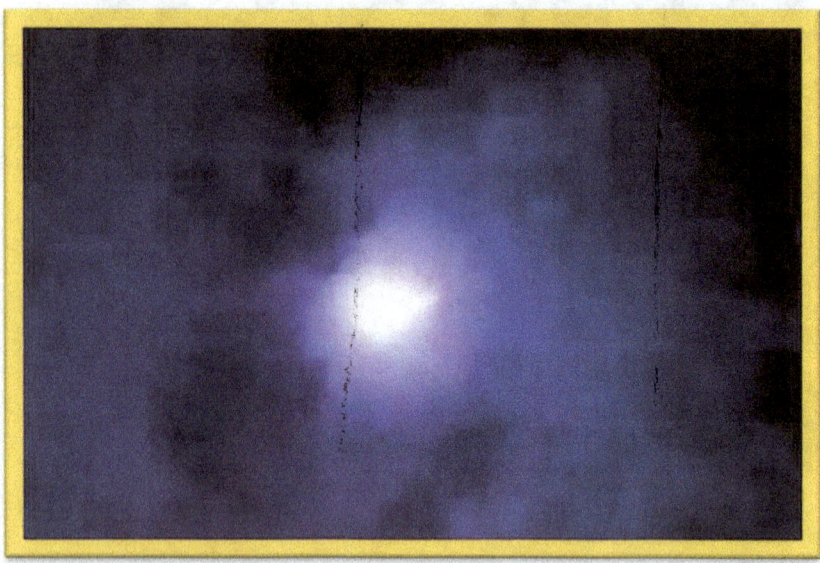

Photo: A bright greenish purple meteor explodes in the night skies over Tokyo, Japan on July 2nd, 2020 releasing over 165 tons of TNT creating a loud sonic boom.

Photo: An incredible view of Jai Ganesh the elephant headed Hindu god of new beginnings near Prescott, Arizona on July 3rd, 2020 while on a drive toward Yarnell, Arizona to visit the memorial to the fallen 19 hot shot firefighters who lost their lives battling a large wildfire.

Photo: Later in the day on July 3rd, 2020 as I was walking my dogs in my neighborhood in Prescott Valley, Arizona this amazing image appeared which to me is unmistakably the head of a lamb. I will forever call this the "Lamb of God" photograph.

Photo: An amazing sunset on July 3rd, 2020 near our former hometown of Grand Haven, Michigan. This was taken by my wife Carol Rose Kloss on a trip back to Michigan to visit friends. Looks like St. Mary knows she's there and is saluting her Rose.

Photo: On the other side of the country on July 3rd, 2020 this amazing sunset appeared near our home in Prescott Valley, Arizona. Earlier in the day my mother Barb and I visited the Garden of Stone at St. Germaine Catholic Church and asked to see an sunset never before seen. Looks like our prayer was answered.

Photo: Another amazing image from July 3rd, 2020 near our home in Prescott Valley, Arizona at sunset. This incredible image shows a single light illuminating one cloud as rain fell on the nearby mountains. This is one of the most beautiful images I've ever seen in nature.

Photo: The Nishino-shima volcano in Japan erupting on July 6th, 2020 sending ash over 27,230 feet into the sky bringing this apocalyptic image of red ash filling the skies.

Photo: Another amazing sunset the evening of July 7th, 2020 near Prescott Valley, Arizona.

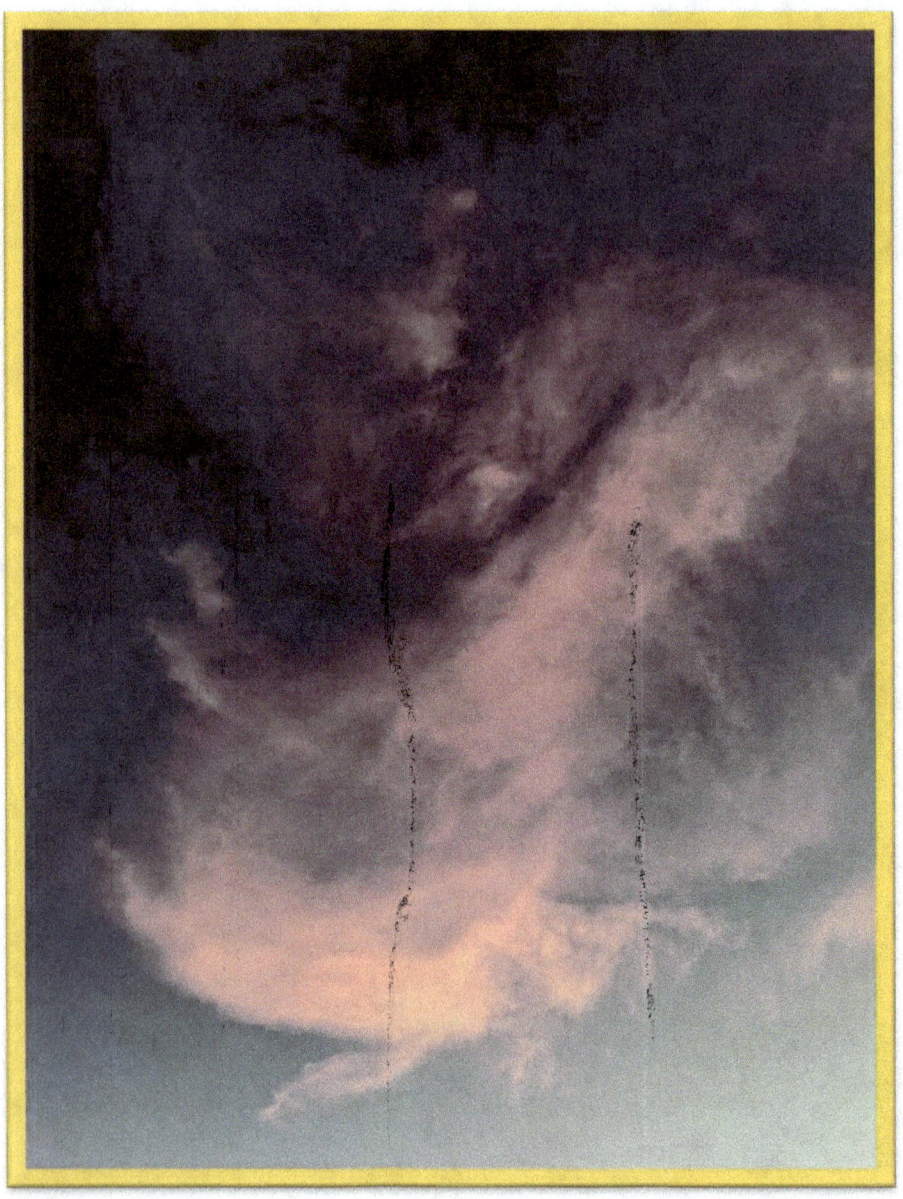

Photo: An amazing sunset in the skies near Prescott Valley, Arizona on July 9th, 2020 after meeting a new friend who is from my home state of Michigan and shares many of the same views as to current political landscapes and civil unrest.

Photo: Another amazing image after a full rosary at exactly 3p.m. on July 9th, 2020 at the Garden of Stone at St. Germaine Catholic Church in Prescott Valley, Arizona. I was praying for our Anunnaki Angels to drive out demon from mankind. This demonic looking face appeared in the clouds at that exact moment in yet another exorcism of another dark entity.

Photo: _Another amazing image from July 10th, 2020 after a full rosary at the Garden of Stone at St. Germaine Catholic Church in Prescott Valley, AZ. I see multiple demonic faces stuck together facing out in different directions. My prayers were focused on driving demons off of the earth so they can no longer possess or influence mankind.

Photo: This image from July 10th, 2020 shows the Kawah Ijen volcano in Indonesia erupting with electric-blue lava that has been attracting crowds of tourists and photographers. The blue light is produced when sulfuric gases come out volcanic cracks and get in touch with the oxygen rich atmospheric air creating a blue flame. What is interesting was I had been having very lucid dreams recently about volcanoes erupting near crowds of onlookers.

Photo: An amazing glimpse of the other kingdom from the sunset of July 10th, 2020. This image is one of the most beautiful I've ever seen in nature.

Photo: Another amazing image from the sunset on July 10th, 2020 which shows what appears to be a figure hovering with its head above the clouds. I found this image quite revealing since my daily prayers have been focused on having our Anunnaki Angels to drive demons out of humans and send them back to An/Heaven/Eden. A demon is a fallen angel to begin with and as long as they renounce Lucifer they could in theory regain their former glory and status in the other kingdom.

Photo: The morning of July 11th, 2020 after a full rosary at Sacred Heart Catholic Church in Prescott, Arizona these twin angel wings appeared out of nowhere in the sky near the Church. The next image will reveal what I found lurking inside the wing to the left in this frame.

Photo: This incredible image from July 11th, 2020 shows the Nishino-Shima volcano in Japan erupting lava bombs creating purple skies with lightning streaking across in a very apocalyptic view from mother nature.

Photo: An amazing image from Flagstaff, Arizona on July 12th, 2020. If you look closely in the bottom middle of the frame there is what appears to be a scowling demonic face.

Photo: Another amazing sunset the evening of July 12th, 2020 brought amazing signs and wonders with it which I will show in the next few photos.

Photo: An amazing image that shows a giant angel wing like cloud covering the skies near Prescott Valley, Arizona on July 12th, 2020 near sunset.

Photo: _Another amazing image from the evening of July 12th, 2020 near Prescott Valley, Arizona at sunset. After a day of prayers for our Annunaki Angel to drive demon off of the earth and out of mankind you can see a very large angel wing here and within it is a face to the bottom left with a cross below it and what looks like a striking serpent or snake in the middle of the wing. More confirmation of my prayers to our father in heaven being heard and answered.

Photo: Another incredible image from the sunset of July 12th, 2020 near our home in Prescott Valley, Arizona shows what appears to me as a large angel wing with faces within it near the top of the frame. This is one of the more breathtaking photos I've ever seen in nature and appeared after a daily rosary asking for this world to disarm, and to turn away from greed.

Photo: Another amazing image from the sunset on July 12th, 2020 near our home in Prescott Valley, Arizona which appears to me as an angel wing carrying away demonic looking faces in the sky.

Photo: This is a close up of the left wing that appeared above Sacred Heart Catholic Church in Prescott, Arizona the morning of July 11th, 2020 after a full rosary asking that our Annunaki Angels drive out demons from humans. If you look closely in the bottom middle of the wing you will see a demonic looking face being carried away. This is a very hopeful image in my opinion as we see the human rights of man being violated under the guise of protecting us from a lethal virus that may have been deliberately released.

Photo: An amazing image of the sunset on July 11th, 2020 near our home in Prescott Valley, Arizona. The purple rains of the monsoon cloud are beautiful beyond words and make me think of the song "Purple Rain" by Prince.

Photo: Another amazing image from the sunset of July 12th, 2020 shows what appears to be some kind of figure with the head of a horse. It is quite beautiful. Could this be the fiery red horse of the apocalypse?

Photo: An amazing image from Prescott Valley, Arizona on July 12th, 2020 shows what appears to me as the face of a bigfoot or sasquatch in the middle left of the frame.

"OUR FATHER ANNUNAKI ADONAI"

The Holy Trinity is described as The Father, The Son, and The Holy Spirit as "one God in three Divine persons." The three persons are distinct, yet are one "substance, essence or nature." In this context, a "nature" is what one is, whereas a "person" is who one is.

The subset of Christianity that accepts this doctrine is known as Trinitarianism. While the developed doctrine of the Trinity is not explicit in the books that are the New Testament, the newer gospels possess a "triadic" understanding of God. I will now show you the face of Our Father or Anunnaki Adonai.

Photo: An incredible photo at sunset near Prescott Valley, Arizona on July 12th, 2020 shows a hanging cloud in the shape of a face. What is unique about this image is during my rosary at 3 p.m. at St. Germaine Catholic Church I asked to see God the Father's face (Annunaki Adonai) in the sky as a sign that Hillel Ben Shachar/Lucifer/Satan/Red Dragon/devil/memnoch/baphomet had been driven off of the earth.

Photo: Another amazing photo from the sunset of July 13th, 2020 near our home in Prescott Valley, Arizona shows this heavenly cloud illuminated by the sunset as it hovers directly above the steeple of a nearby church. This is also one of the most beautiful images I've ever seen.

Photo: Another amazing cloud formation in the form of a horse head on July 13th, 2020 near Prescott Valley, Arizona. The ears and eye are quite unmistakable. I again think of the line from The Doors song "I can't see your face in my mind" with the prophetic lyric "insanity's horse adorns the sky." I cannot think of a greater time in history of people going insane from all the unlawful restrictions placed on humans due to the release of what most likely was a designed bioweapon with the COVID-19 coronavirus. Does the appearance of three horse heads as clouds reinforce that we have now seen the three riders of the horsemen of the apocalypse?

Photo: An amazing image from the sunset of July 13th, 2020 near Prescott Valley, Arizona and what appears to me as a fish like figure with a human like face and mouth wide open.

Photo: An incredible image from sunset on July 13th, 2020 near Prescott Valley, Arizona and what appears to me as a devil or demon dancing near the top of the steeple. This image is so remarkable to me in that you can clearly see a tail, legs, arms/wings, and a clearly defined face that seems to be smiling. The demon also appears to have the head of a male figure with handlebar mustache in its mouth.

Photo: Another amazing image from sunset on July 13th, 2020 in what appears to be a demonic looking figure staring down toward the earth.

Photo: An amazing image from the afternoon of July 13th, 2020 and what appears to be some kind of figure biting into a cloud.

Photo: An amazing image of an angel wing above St. Germaine Catholic Church in Prescott Valley, Arizona the morning of July 13th, 2020 during a full rosary for world peace and for the world to turn away from greed.

Photo: An amazing image of a mysterious face in the clouds above St. Germaine Catholic Church in Prescott Valley, Arizona the morning of July 13th, 2020. I did not get the feeling this was a threatening entity, but rather a protective entity of very high order from the other kingdom.

Photo: An amazing image of the sunset near our home in Prescott Valley, Arizona on July 15th, 2020 shows what appears to me as a mother elephant following two baby elephants. It is beautiful beyond words.

Photo: An incredible image from the morning of July 16th, 2020 shows a cloud figure with arms outstretched above the Garden of Stone at St. Germaine Catholic Church in Prescott Valley, Arizona during a full rosary for world peace and for the world to turn away from greed.

Photo: An incredible image from the morning of July 16th, 2020 shows an angel cloud wing directly above the stone figure of Christ in the Garden of Stone at St. Germaine Catholic Church in Prescott Valley, Arizona during a full rosary for world peace and for the world to turn away from greed.

Photo: Another amazing image from St. Germaine Catholic Church and the Garden of Stone showing what appears to be yet another glimpse of Jai Ganesh the elephant headed Hindu god of new beginnings on July 16th, 2020.

Photo: Another amazing image of what appears to me as the head of a bear that appeared above the Garden of Stone at St. Germaine Catholic Church on July 16th, 2020 after a rosary for world peace and for the world to turn away from greed.

Photo: An incredible image of what appears to me as "The Angel of The Lord" that appeared directly above the roof of our home in Prescott Valley, Arizona on July 16th, 2020 after a full rosary at St. Germaine Catholic Church for world peace and for the world to turn away from greed. The second I snapped this photo the cloud began to rumble loudly with thunder. If you look closely enough on the right wing you can see a bird diving down from the sky. I will enclose a blow up of this bird in the next image. When I see this image the song "Learn to Fly" by the Foo Fighters comes to mind. In that song Annunaki Angel half-breed Dave Grohl sings "I'm looking to the sky to save me, looking for a sign of life, looking for something help me burn out bright."

Photo: A close up image of a diving bird that appears to me to look like the Holy Spirit (paraclete) along the leading edge of the right wing on the Angel of The Lord from July 16th, 2020.

Photo: An incredible image from July 17th, 2020 directly above our home in Prescott Valley, Arizona shows what appears to be an angel in the cloud to the left holding a very large angel wing chasing a demonic face/mask to the right that appears to be fleeing and shrieking and crashing head first into another demonic looking face/mask. This came after a morning rosary/mass at St. Germaine Catholic Church in Prescott Valley, Arizona where my prayers were focused on world peace and for the world to turn from greed and for our Annunaki angels to drive demons off of the earth.

Photo: This beautiful rainbow appeared on July 17th, 2020 near Sedona, Arizona on the exact date of my wife Carol Rose's and I's 12th wedding anniversary. There is not doubt this is the other kingdom saying hello to the New Wine and New Rose.

Photo: The beautiful sunset the evening of July 17th, 2020 near Sedona, Arizona as my wife Carol Rose and I celebrated our 12th wedding anniversary.

Photo: The comet Neowise passes in our skies on July 18th, 2020 at 144,000 m.p.h. or 40 miles per second. My half-brother James who the world knew as Jim Morrison, lead singer of The Doors and I used to refer to these celestial bodies as "horses." In fact, in the Doors song "The Soft Parade" the song ends with both of us singing "if all else fails we can whip the horses' eyes and make them sleep and cry." What we are both saying here is if our warnings from The New Wine are unheeded for the world to turn away from war and greed we can possibly, through daily prayer, change the trajectory of these "horses" of the apocalypse by causing them change course by "whipping their eyes" to make them "sleep and cry" (miss their target of crashing into the fallen planet of earth ruled by paganism, idolatry, and greed).

Photo: An amazing image from the Garden of Stone at St. Germaine Catholic Church in Prescott Valley, Arizona on July 19th, 2020 during morning mass and a full rosary for world peace and for the world to turn away from greed. What I see here in this image looks like an angel face in the middle right of the frame with hair flowing up to the left in the sky. It is quite beautiful.

Photo: An incredible image of a very unusual looking cloud formation the afternoon of July 19th, 2020 near our home in Prescott Valley, Arizona. It is difficult to determine what is occurring here weather-wise or spiritually, but it was a very powerful sight of our Father's presence in nature.

Photo: An incredible image from July 19th, 2020 after an afternoon rosary for world peace and for Annunaki angel to drive demon out of mankind and off of the earth this very demonic looking figure appeared which appears to be smiling and staring towards the lower right frame.

Photo: An incredible sunset the evening of July 19th, 2020 near Prescott Valley, Arizona and yet another glimpse of the other kingdom.

Photo: The incredibly beautiful sunset on July 20th, 2020 near our home in Prescott Valley, Arizona brought with it some amazing signs and wonders which I will document below with photos.

Photo: Another incredibly beautiful view to the east of clouds being illuminated by the setting sun near Prescott Valley, Arizona on July 20th, 2020.

Photo: An incredible image from the setting sun on July 20th, 2020 near Prescott Valley, Arizona shows what appears to me as a dancing elephant.

Photo: Another incredible image of the setting sun near Prescott Valley, Arizona on July 20th, 2020 shows this very mysterious formation in the clouds which to me appears to be yet another representation of the concept of "infinity" with two circles being joined together.

Photo: Another amazing image of the clouds setting at sunset near Prescott Valley, Arizona on July 20th, 2020 shows this very ghostly looking face.

Photo: This amazing image from the setting sun near Prescott Valley, Arizona on July 20th, 2020 shows what appears to me as an image within an image. Specifically, I see both the head of a deer and also the head of a demon or devil with horns.

Photo: An amazing image of the sun rising across Mingus Mountain near our home in Prescott Valley, Arizona on July 21st, 2020. I found this image amazing because it was the same day my favorite director Oliver Stone's autobiography "Chasing The Light" was released worldwide.

Photo: An amazing view of the setting sun as monsoon storm clouds roll in near our home in Prescott Valley, Arizona on July 24th, 2020. This is one of the most beautiful images I've ever seen in nature.

Photo: The morning of July 25th, 2020 at the Garden of Stone at St. Germaine Catholic Church in Prescott Valley, Arizona during a rosary for world peace and for the world to turn away from greed this incredibly beautiful angel wing appeared above the church steeple.

Photo: The morning of July 25th, 2020 during a rosary for world peace and for the world to turn away from greed this cloud in the shape of a cross appeared directly above the Garden of Stone at St. Germaine Catholic Church in Prescott Valley, Arizona.

Photo: The morning of July 25th, 2020 at the Garden of Stone at St. Germaine Catholic Church in Prescott Valley, Arizona this enormous Arch Angel wing appeared as the sun rays bend towards the earth.

Photo: An incredible image from the evening of July 25th, 2020 shows the setting sun near our home in Prescott Valley, Arizona.

Photo: An incredible image of a face looking upwards towards the heavens near Payson, Arizona on July 26th, 2020 as my wife Carol Rose and I visited Tonto Natural Bridge State Park.

Photo: This incredible "spirit cloud" appeared directly above our home in Prescott Valley, Arizona on July 26th, 2020. I see numerous faces within this cloud.

Photo: Apocalyptic lightning crashes near the Washington monument in Washington, D.C. on July 24th, 2020 leaving onlookers to describe it as some of the most powerful lightning they had ever seen.

Photo: An amazing view of the comet "Neowise" streaking across the night sky past earth at 17,500 m.p.h. in July 2020. The green trail is beyond beautiful. The amazing thing about this celestial body is it won't pass earth again for another 6,800 years. It is amazing how long these space rocks can travel through the solar system untouched.

"AN ANGELIC APOCALYPSE"

There is no doubt tremendous anxiety surrounding the word "Apocalypse." Most associate this term with the total destruction of life on the planet. Let's look at other definitions. One of the Jewish and Christian writings of 200 B.C. to A.D. 150 described apocalypse as marked by pseudonymity, symbolic imagery, and the expectation of an imminent cosmic cataclysm in which God destroys the ruling powers of evil and raises the righteous to life in a messianic kingdom. I submit this proposition: is it possible to have such a messianic kingdom here on earth despite all the world's problems of wars, famines, disease, and natural disasters? Let's again look at some current apocalyptic signs, which may help shape and foster such a kingdom of light. I have provided numerous images in this book to show the spiritual wars waged in our skies between angels and demons. Let's look at other events occurring simultaneously.

On August 1st, 2020, a 6.4 magnitude earthquake struck the Philippines and a 5.7 magnitude earthquake, followed by a stronger

6.0 magnitude earthquake struck Papua New Guinea as powerful eruptions from the Nishinoshima volcano in Japan erupted. Also, on August 1st, 2020 headlines read "potentially dangerous asteroid the size of football pitch will fly close to earth on 8th." The article described the asteroid traveling at a break neck speed of 13.4 kilometers per second, and that the celestial body won't return to earth until 2137.

On August 2nd, 2020, a 5.8 magnitude earthquake struck near Papua New Guinea.

On August 2nd and August 3rd, 2020, the Langila volcano in Papua New Guinea erupted for the first time since 2018.

On August 3rd, 2020, a huge blue/green fireball lit up the skies in New Mexico. On August 1st and 4th, 2020, two 5.7 magnitude earthquakes struck Vanuatu. Also, on August 4th, 2020, a 5.8 magnitude earthquake struck near Guatemala.

Photo: On August 1st, 2020 after a morning rosary at the Garden of Stone at St. Germaine Catholic Church in Prescott Valley, Arizona asking for more signs and wonders in the skies this amazing animal head cloud formation was directly above our home at noon.

Photo: On August 1st, 2020 after a morning rosary at the Garden of Stone at St. Germaine Catholic Church in Prescott Valley, Arizona asking for more signs and wonders in the skies this amazing angel wing cloud formation appeared at noon near our home.

Photo: This amazing angel spirit cloud appeared near our home in Prescott Valley, Arizona on August 1st, 2020.

Photo: Another incredible angel spirit cloud near Prescott Valley, Arizona on August 1st, 2020.

Photo: The Nishinoshima island volcano in a powerful eruption on August 1st, 2020. Coincidentally, I had just completed a rosary at the Garden of Sone at St. Germaine Catholic Church in Prescott Valley, Arizona asking for daily demonstrations of true king authority in the form of earthquakes, volcanoes, hurricanes, cyclones, derechos, tornadoes, meteors, asteroids, tsunamis, wildfires and floods until this world disarms all weapons of mass destruction and turns away from idolatry and greed.

Photo: Another incredibly beautiful angel spirit cloud above our home in Prescott Valley, Arizona on August 1st, 2020 at exactly 3 p.m.

Photo: Another incredible angel spirit cloud formation near our home above Prescott Valley, Arizona at exactly 3 p.m. on August 1st, 2020.

Photo: On August 1st, 2020 at 3 p.m. this incredible cloud formation appeared directly above our home in Prescott Valley, Arizona. I call this image "angels kissing." If you look closely, you can see a demonic face between the two kissing angels. My prayers earlier in the day had been focused on having our Anunnaki Angels drive demons out of mankind and off of the earth using our two keys of "Be Love" and "Believe."

Photo: Another incredible image of a face in a cloud high above Prescott Valley, Arizona on August 1st, 2020 after another rosary at the Garden of Stone at St. Germaine Catholic Church.

Photo: An incredibly beautiful sunset the night of August 1st, 2020 above Prescott Valley, Arizona. This is no doubt a glimpse of the other kingdom.

Photo: An incredibly beautiful sunset the night of August 1st, 2020 above Prescott Valley, Arizona. This is no doubt a glimpse of the other kingdom and what appears to me as a crown of a king.

Photo: An incredibly beautiful sunset the night of August 1st, 2020 above Prescott Valley, Arizona. This is no doubt a glimpse of the other kingdom and the view of the moon behind red clouds is amazing and spectacular.

Photo: An amazingly beautiful sunset the evening of August 2nd, 2020 brought this incredible red sun with it and some amazing images of more angels and demons I will show below.

Photo: At sunset on August 2nd, 2020 this incredible image appeared which if you look closely to the right you will see an angel face staring forward in flight with a demonic face behind it.

Photo: A close up of the brighter angel facing off against the demonic looking devil from August 2nd, 2020. The incredible thing about this image was my wife was shopping earlier and her total at the register was $66.77 to which she jokingly made a comment to the cashier "I'm half angel and half devil." Seems like St. Mary heard her comment and is responding in kind.

Photo: Another amazing view of the angel in flight with the bright moon to the bottom left of the screen on the evening of August 2nd, 2020.

Photo: An incredible photo of the face of some kind of beast while on a walk in my neighborhood near Prescott Valley, Arizona on August 4th, 2020.

Photo: Another amazing image of some kind of face with eyes forming the symbol for infinity above our home near Prescott Valley, Arizona on August 4th, 2020.

Photo: An amazing sunset the evening of August 4th, 2020 near Prescott Valley, Arizona.

Photo: Another incredibly beautiful view of the sunset near Prescott Valley, Arizona on August 4th, 2020.

Photo: An incredible angel wing cloud the evening of August 4th, 2020 near Prescott Valley, Arizona.

Photo: An incredible view of an entity in flight towards the heavens with very specific and defined facial features taken on the evening of August 4th, 2020.

On August 5th, 2020 a 6.4 magnitude earthquake struck near Vanuatu as tropical storm Isaias left 2.2 million homes and businesses without power in N.J. as it scraped the northeast coast.

Also, on August 5th, 2020, the Suwanosejima volcano erupted. On August 6th, 2020, a 6.3 magnitude earthquake struck near South Africa and a 4.8 magnitude earthquake struck near Puerto Rico.

On August 7th, 2020, a 5.1 magnitude earthquake struck Russia, as a 5.0 magnitude earthquake struck Peru and a 5.3 magnitude earthquake struck China.

On August 8th, 2020, the Sinabung volcano erupted, sending ash 2,000 meters into the air, and a 5.5 magnitude earthquake struck near Alaska. Also, on August 8th, 2020, massive flooding in southern China engulfed huge swathes of farmland.

Photo: An amazing sunset the evening of August 5th, 2020 near our home in Prescott Valley, Arizona.

Photo: _On August 7th, 2020 while driving in my new hometown of Prescott Valley, Arizona I saw a black truck with this symbol. This is a red and black pentagram and is the chief symbol of the dark fallen angel Lucifer/Hillel Ben Shachar/Memnoch/Satan/red dragon/devil/baphomet and definitive proof of major spiritual combat in the modern world.

Photo: The incredibly beautiful sunset of August 7th, 2020 near our home in Prescott Valley, Arizona shows what appears as a huge wing in the background next to grazing cattle.

Photo: Another beautiful view of grazing cattle as the suns rays streak over them the evening of August 7th, 2020.

Photo: Another amazing angel cloud the morning of August 8th, 2020 near Prescott Valley, Arizona.

Photo: Another amazing angel cloud the morning of August 8th, 2020 near Prescott Valley, Arizona.

Photo: An amazing angel cloud the morning of August 8th, 2020 near Prescott Valley, Arizona. The top cloud appears to me as a shark.

Photo: An amazing angel cloud the morning of August 8th, 2020 near Prescott Valley, Arizona with what appears to me as an angel arm out swimming from the above shark in the middle of the frame.

Photo: An incredible image from The Garden of Stone at St. Germaine Catholic Church in Prescott Valley, Arizona on August 8th, 2020 shows what appears to be a face smiling with joy looking up into the heavens above.

Photo: Another amazing view at The Garden of Stone at St. Germaine Catholic Church in Prescott Valley, Arizona on August 8th, 2020 shows an amazing image of what appears as a face in a cloud looking to the left of the frame.

Photo: An amazing view from The Garden of Stone at St. Germaine Catholic Church in Prescott Valley, Arizona on August 8th, 2020 shows what appears to be the face of some kind of creature staring to the right of the frame.

On August 9th, 2020 a 5.1 magnitude earthquake struck North Carolina setting a record as the strongest earthquake in 94 years as flooding killed seven people in Greece. Also, on August 9th, 2020 a 5.7 magnitude earthquake struck Alaska as a 5.9 magnitude earthquake struck near South Africa.

On August 10th, 2020, a 5.7 magnitude earthquake struck near Honduras, as headlines read, "severe storms bring large hail, damaging winds, torrential rain to the Twin Cities metro area."

Also, on August 10th, 2020, a rare derecho storm that lasted 14 hours straight hit the Midwest with 100 m.p.h. winds, knocking out power for 1 million customers. Also, on August 10th, 2020 headlines read "U.S., China in last-ditch effort to avoid war at sea."

On August 11th, 2020, a powerful derecho with category 2 hurricane force 140 m.p.h. winds struck farmland in Iowa for 14 hours, causing massive damage to silos, farms and homes.

Photo: On August 10th, 2020 a new angel statue arrived after we decided to decorate our lawn with this divine messenger. We named this statue Angel Matilda in honor of someone special who is helping promote The New Wine series of books to help raise funds for her brain surgery. Needless to say our chocolate lab pointer mix Reese seemed to take to this new friend immediately.

Photo: On August 10th, 2020 Mt. Sinabung in Indonesia erupted sending ash over three miles into the air.

Photo: An amazing sunset the evening of August 11th, 2020 near Prescott Valley, Arizona after a daily rosary for world peace and for the world to turn away from war and greed.

On August 12th, 2020 a 6.0 magnitude earthquake struck near Tanzania in East Africa as a 5.5 magnitude earthquake struck the Philippines, a 5.7 magnitude earthquake struck Alaska, a 5.6 magnitude earthquake struck Pakistan, and a 5.0 magnitude earthquake struck Russia.

On August 14th, 2020, a 5.3 magnitude earthquake struck off the coast of Mexico and a 5.8 magnitude earthquake struck off of the coast of Chile.

On August 15th, 2020, a 5.1 magnitude earthquake struck near Chile. On August 16th, 2020, a 5.2 magnitude earthquake struck in the Philippines and a 5.7 magnitude earthquake struck near Alaska.

Also, on August 16th, 2020 a truck sized asteroid passed by the earth at over 27,500 m.p.h. within 2,000 miles and it wasn't discovered until after it passed. This was the closest in history an asteroid has come to the earth without hitting it.

On August 17th, 2020 a 5.4 magnitude earthquake struck near Trinidad and a 5.3 magnitude earthquake struck near New Guinea.

Also, on August 17th, 2020, a very strong 6.7 magnitude earthquake struck the Philippines, and a 5.1 magnitude earthquake struck Baja, California, as a 5.8 magnitude earthquake struck near Madagascar.

Photo: An amazing angel cloud formation above the Catalina Mountains near Tucson, Arizona on August 12th, 2020 while visiting local retina surgeons to work with them on visualization during retina surgery. To the left I see an angel like figure with arms outstretched and to the right I see an angel with head bowed and wings folded on its back. It was quite a comforting and beautiful sight.

Photo: An incredible image of mysterious clouds at sunset near Tucson, Arizona on August 12th, 2020. I see two ominous looking faces to the right of the frame.

Photo: An incredible image of two angel wings floating in the skies above Tucson, Arizona the morning of August 13th, 2020 appearing as I was on my way to work with local retina surgeons assisting them with visualization during surgery.

Photo: An incredible image of an angel wing floating in the skies above Tucson, Arizona the morning of August 13th, 2020 appearing as I was on my way to work with local retina surgeons assisting them with visualization during surgery.

Photo: An incredible image of an angel wing floating in the skies above Tucson, Arizona the morning of August 13th, 2020 appearing as I was on my way to work with local retina surgeons assisting them with visualization during surgery.

Photo: An incredible image of an angel wing floating in the skies above Tucson, Arizona the morning of August 13th, 2020 appearing as I was on my way to work with local retina surgeons assisting them with visualization during surgery.

Photo: An incredible image of an all-seeing eye with an angel floating in the skies above Tucson, Arizona the morning of August 13th, 2020 appearing as I was on my way to work with local retina surgeons assisting them with visualization during surgery.

Photo: An incredible image from the evening of August 13th, 2020 shows what appears to me as very large angel wing carrying away a demonic scowling face with it. My recent prayers had been for Anunnaki angels to drive demons out of humans.

Photo: Another amazing image from the evening of August 13th, 2020 shows what appears to me as a angelic face staring down from the heavens.

Photo: Another amazing image from the evening of August 13th, 2020 shows what appears to me as a figure floating in the skies above Prescott Valley, Arizona.

Photo: An incredibly beautiful sunset above Prescott Valley, Arizona on August 13th, 2020.

Photo: On August 16th, 2020 more than 2,500 powerful lightning strikes streaked across the skies above San Francisco, California.

Photo: On the evening of August 17th, 2020 my wife Carol Rose and I said a prayer together for success in delivering the incredible message behind our New Wine series of books that seek to bring peace and hope to the world. Within minutes a major rainstorm hit our neighborhood producing a rainbow and this incredible image of a storm cloud with a golden angelic looking face to the top right of the frame.

On August 18th, 2020, two strong 6.8 and 6.9 magnitude earthquakes struck near Indonesia, and a 4.2 magnitude earthquake struck near Willits, CA.

Also on August 18th, 2020, California Governor Newsome declared a statewide emergency in response to a historic heat wave, sustained high winds and wildfires.

On August 19th, 2020, a 4.8 magnitude earthquake struck near Death Valley, CA, and a 5.4 magnitude earthquake struck off the coast of Columbia. From August 16-19th, 2020 10,849 lightning strikes over 72 hours sparked 367 wildfires in northern California with over 300 acres that have burned, forcing thousands to evacuate their homes.

On August 20th, 2020, a 5.0 magnitude struck near Alaska. On August 31st, 2020, a 6.8 magnitude earthquake struck near Chile. On September 5th, 2020, another 6.3 magnitude earthquake struck near Chile.

On September 5th, 2020, a 6.2 magnitude earthquake struck near Vanuatu. On September 5th, 2020, a 6.7 magnitude earthquake struck near Brazil.

On September 6th, 2020, a 6.3 magnitude earthquake struck near the Philippines, as another 6.0 magnitude earthquake struck near Vanuatu. As of August 2020, there have been nine named tropical storms in the year, which is a meteorological record, with Josephine being the earliest named "J" storm ever.

Photo: An incredibly radiant sunrise from the other kingdom on the morning of August 19th, 2020 while in my way to work with local retina surgeons in Phoenix, Arizona.

Photo: An amazing angel cloud wing the morning of August 19th, 2020 near Phoenix, Arizona while on my way to work with local retina surgeons.

Photo: An incredibly mysterious looking cloud formation the afternoon of August 19th, 2020 near Prescott Valley, Arizona. This cloud looks to me like a mushroom cloud from a nuclear blast. I am hoping and praying this is a warning from the other kingdom the entire world will heed.

Photo: Wildfires burned thousands of acres and destroyed thousands of buildings on August 20th, 2020 in what seems like an apocalyptic event of record heat, lightning, and fires.

Photo: An incredible satellite image shows the smoke from the wildfires in northern California moving over 600 miles off the coast into the Pacific Ocean on August 20th, 2020.

Photo: An amazing view of the setting sun turning red on the evening of August 20th, 2020 near our home in Prescott Valley, Arizona.

Photo: An incredible image of what appears to be an "all seeing eye" in the sky on the evening of August 20th, 2020 near our home in Prescott Valley, Arizona.

Photo: An incredible image of what appears as an ominous face in the clouds above Prescott Valley, Arizona on the evening of August 20th, 2020.

Photo: An incredible image of what appears as an angelic cloud hovering over the setting sun the evening of August 23rd, 2020 near our home in Prescott Valley, Arizona.

Photo: An amazing image of an angel hovering in a cloud above Prescott Valley, Arizona on August 23rd, 2020.

Photo: An amazing photo of a huge angel wing covering the entire skies directly above our home in Prescott Valley, Arizona on August 23rd, 2020.

Photo: An extraordinary image of what appears as an angel and a demon having a heated exchange in the skies above Prescott Valley, Arizona on August 23rd, 2020.

Photo: An extraordinary image of a figure with his arm outstretched as if reaching for something on the evening of August 23rd, 2020 near Prescott Valley, Arizona.

Photo: An incredible image of what appears as glowing eyes above a church steeple near our home in Prescott Valley, Arizona the evening of August 23rd, 2020.

Photo: An incredible image from the evening of August 30th, 2020 shows what appears as a glowing angelic face starting towards the ground.

Photo: An incredible view of the setting sun near San Diego, California as wildfires raged nearby the evening of September 5th, 2020. What is amazing about this photo is my wife took this with her camera and I could not duplicate the same sun rays shooting to the top right and top left with my camera even though I was at the same vantage point.

Photo: Raging apocalyptic wildfires near the mountains east of San Diego on Labor Day Weekend 2020 as my wife and I visited local beaches for vacation.

Photo: We arrived safely back in Arizona after short weekend vacation in California where wildfires raged. This amazing image of an angel appeared directly above our home near Prescott Valley,

Photo: Another amazing image of what appears as an angel flying sideways directly above our home near Prescott Valley, Arizona on September 7th, 2020.

Photo: Another amazing image of an angel in flight from the evening of September 7th, 2020 near Prescott Valley, Arizona.

To date, the COVID-19 coronavirus, which seems to have genesis near Wuhan, China, and may have been a designed biological weapon, has killed hundreds of thousands of people worldwide and affected millions resulting in the U.S. Congress passing a $2.2 trillion dollar stimulus bill geared towards small businesses and middle-class wage earners.

Soon after the coronavirus outbreak five African nations experienced swarms of crop eating locusts. Recent headlines read "over 120,000 weather records broken in 2019."

On May 5th, 2020 headlines read, "Coronavirus threatens new 'cold war' between the United States and China, as virus spurs collapse in relations."

On June 16th, 2020 headlines read "North Korea blows up a liaison office in Kaesong used for talks with South Korea" as North Korean leaders threatened to deploy troops into the DMZ.

Also, on June 16th, 2020 headlines read: "twenty Indian Army troops were killed in a clash with Chinese soldiers along the countries' disputed borders."

These events would definitely fall under the prophecy given by Jesus Christ, that prior to his return there would be "wars and rumors of wars."

Photo: An artist's rendering of the four horsemen of the Apocalypse from the prophetic Book of Revelations.

From Revelation 6:1-2: "I watched as the Lamb opened the first of the seven seals, and there was before me a white horse, its rider held a bow, and he was given a crown, and he rode out as a conqueror bent on a conquest."

At first glance this passage appears to signal Jesus Christ as the rider on the white horse, but further introspection reveals that the Lamb (Jesus Christ) opened the seal, and that this rider on the white horse is a "Trojan horse" who appears to be doing the work of God, but is really "bent on a conquest" and has great wealth and power to enact his will upon the people, all the while claiming to be working for God.

Revelation 6:3-4: "When the Lamb opened the second seal, another horse came out, a fiery red one. Its rider was given power to take peace from the earth and force men to slay each other. To him was given a large sword." This fiery red horse obviously refers to the "wars and Rumors of wars" from Revelation, and is consistent with the events we are seeing take place in and around China.

Revelation 6:5-6: "When the Lamb opened the third seal, I looked and there was before me a black horse. Its rider held a pair of scales in his hand, saying, a quart of wheat for a day's wages, and three quarts of barley for a day's wages, and do not damage the oil and the wine." This is clearly a reference to famine and also a reference to "wine" as in the title of The New Wine series of books.

Revelation 6:7-8: "And I looked and there was before me a pale horse. Its rider was named Death, and Hades was following close behind him. They were given power over a fourth of the earth to kill by sword, famine and plaque, and the wild beasts of the earth." This passage clearly referencing the warnings from Fatima of the consequences both physical and spiritual of waging wars on the earth with modern weapons. This passage also predicts how famine and disease (think COVID-19) bring death, which will be like hell for many.

I want to take the time here to divulge a piece of information I have not yet shared in any volumes of The New Wine. Shortly before moving from Michigan to Arizona, I met in person with an individual I've known since I was a teenager. This man lives in Christian ministry. I told him on more than one occasion that I had received the message "more are dying" around the summer of 2017, less than three years before the outbreak of the coronavirus or COVID-19. This clearly was a message from the other kingdom, which has now been proven to be prophetic. To date, more than 600,000 deaths have been attributed to this pandemic. I spoke with my cousin, who recently retired from the U.S. Army as an officer and we both agree this virus was likely a designed bioweapon.

Photo: The Office of the Staff Judge Advocate U.S. Army, Fort Polk, Louisiana in the summer of 2000, right before my honorable discharge from active duty.

I was recalled from the Individual Ready Reserves in early 2004, after it appeared the Iraq War would be longer than expected. I was inexplicably discharged on February 19th, 2004 seven days before my 30th birthday, which I can only attribute to a spinal cord injury I received on active duty.

I am at the top right, just below the tank turret. Colonel Christopher M. Maher, current lead counsel to the Inspector General of the United States (seated center first row), was recruited to guard the Tomb of the Unknown, a very high military honor, and also as a Blackhawk pilot.

I opted not re-enlist, as I sensed another possible Vietnam type of war on the horizon. I definitely saw many odd and conflicting things on our military base during this time, including Special Forces soldiers from Eastern Bloc nations training in special ops on an American military base, as well as Russian made Sikorsky helicopters flying over mock Middle Eastern villages on our base, which was also known as the Joint Readiness Training Center. Ft. Polk trained Navy S.E.A.L.s and Army Ranger Units to include Delta Force before deployment to Iraq.

Photo: A lean and mean U.S. Army JAG member Specialist Matthew Douglas Pinard (top right under tank turret) standing next to good friend Specialist Richard Funkhouser circa 2000 at Fort Polk, Louisiana, Joint Readiness Training Center. Both SPC Pinard and SPC Funkhouser had family members that were Special Forces Officers who saw combat duty in Iraq.

There were many odd occurrences I witnessed on the base that led me to believe the middle east was being targeted for invasion prior to 9/11. My Master's Degree thesis on the Vietnam

War and pacification at Louisiana State University during this time was called "one of the best" he's ever read by Military History Professor Stanley Hilton who is the author of "Hitler's Secret War in South America." I was rated as an expert marksman with the M-16A2 as I hit 39/40 pop up targets up to 400 meters away on the rifle range in basic training and likely would have been assigned to an combat infantry unit during the Iraq War had I not been honorably discharged.

Photo: An official copy of my Army Achievement Medal signed July 25th, 2000 by Colonel Gregory Lynch at Fort Polk, Louisiana for "exceptionally meritorious service with devotion to duty, dedication to mission and selfless service reflecting great credit upon himself, his unit and The United States Army." It is difficult to comprehend that a few years later our military would be embroiled in the invasion of a nation under manufactured and false pretenses.

Photo: An undated photo of the late James Douglas Morrison, lead singer of The Doors, with poet and good friend Michael McClure. As I stated in the previous volumes of The New Wine, I believe I am the reincarnation of James Douglas Morrison. I have the same middle name, the same mole on my left cheek, knew all the Doors lyrics before I heard them, and can hit every note Jim recorded. I actually believe we are St. Mary's conjoined fraternal twins, in which Jim referred to us as "lurking jaws, joints in time." What is humorous to me is that my wife Carol Rose (who is neither a Jim Morrison or Doors fan) saw this photo and said to me, "when did you have a beard?" I said to her, "when I was lead singer of The Doors."

I will pose the same question I asked in The New Wine: Volume III 'The Veil Rent,' does anyone dispute we are in the Book of Revelations and in The Apocalypse? Does no one want a world where people are equally fed and clothed, a world where wealth is distributed evenly, a world where actual weapons of mass destruction (like greed, war, poverty, disease, nuclear and biological weapons) were removed? To date, there are 747 billionaires in the United States alone, and nine private individuals control 95% of the world's wealth. Eight sovereign states have successfully detonated nuclear weapons. The arms race has not slowed down, but rather increased exponentially. This planet will not survive a third world war. One might actually say this is one of those "come to Jesus" type of moments. These facts alone support the need for Kingdom Come.

"The barns have stormed, the windows kept, and only one of all the rest to dance and save us from the divine mockery of words..." - James Douglas Morrison

The New Revelations of Beasts

A new original poem by Matthew Douglas Pinard and James Douglas Morrison

Behold, an incandescent red breasted beast with seven horns and ten heads seven diadems, jeweled crowns of a fallen celestial being claiming to be king the dark river Sons revved up as a deuce in a crown of three sing hail to the thief, trust in the night, a young Aydan bright as moon light

    Says he believes and is granted one of two keys unlocking the Queen, who lays down a Council of Nicea, giving one creed that drives seven beasts' heads into clouded pillows not woven with threads, revealing the one who is truly dead and not resurrected in belief and not in love with three only begotten Sons

    A naval brigade bearing weapons of mass destruction plots a course past stars into a South China Sea with long range missiles, arrows as deadly as a red dragon sun. The ring of fire is cracked open, oscillating terrestrial crusts, bringing her fire through the mantle and veil, sounding seven horns of eternal peace

    Reminding us all, there is one above who is beyond our reproach and is only love, and is every molecule of light inside our flaming stars and suns who knows our mitochondrial DNA down to every last strand, and as he shakes his fist and hand two Fujita fives touchdown simultaneously in a union of magnolias

    An amazing display of true king authority rips open the hearts, minds and Higgs Boson atoms of world leaders collapsing knees as tongues confess the incarnate lamb has not ever been dead and now commands a golden fleet of winged women and men immortal newborn half breeds that rule with twin keys

    True kingdom angels and saints in a hair's breadth drop down from wormholes past stars and suns to bring this world to genuflect enforcing true king peace mandated by the woman clothed in the sun who first came to children tending to a flock of sheep on a hillside in Spain as she relinquished the dancing sun

    To the earth and proclaimed my Prince of Peace and His Paraclete have won in two thousand twenty ushers in an invisible sun of disarmament in lieu of dismemberment, as nations wielding actual WMDs devolve instantly into love and become one world inseminated with her tangential keys lent from above

    And like Christ Cornell's stone, I'll wait for you there and in the meantime give birth to seven Peace Towns inside, seven mothers, seven brides of the Father for pearls and swine bereft of me. Long and weary, my road has been. I am not your carpet ride, I am the sky, I am the lightning, I am his light.

Ego Sum Via, Et Veritas, Et Vita

In this thrilling fourth volume of The New Wine, author Matthew Douglas Pinard delves further into "other kingdom" mysteries as he dissects the secrets surrounding the sealed messages delivered by Our Lady of Fatima, and uses incredible photos to demonstrate which chapter of the Book of Revelations we are currently in.

This astounding book contains amazingly beautiful photos of sunsets and sunrises never before seen, as well as actual images of spiritual entities, angels and demons in battle in the heavens above. The author further expounds on how the current tension between the United States and China in the South China Seas may lead to a great and final conflict as well as premonitions he received relating to the outbreak of the deadly coronavirus.

The author answers questions such as "who is the red breasted beast" described in the ancient prophecy of the Woman Clothed in the Sun?

What was the series of messages given to three young children by St. Mary in Fatima, Spain in 1917, and what relevance does it hold to today's world?

- Are there current signs of the apocalypse in today's world?
- Do UFOs exist, and is this evidence of "other worlds?"
- Who are the modern-day prophets in recent music history?
- What happens to the spirit when we die?
- How do angels and demons manifest in our world, and can they influence our natural environment?
- What do we mean when we say "celestial body?"
- What does the face of the Father (Anunnaki Adonai) look like?
- What is the "flaming sword" of the apocalypse?
- What is the "Holy Spirit paraclete" and how does it manifest in our world?
- What does the lyric "insanity's horse adorns the sky" from the famous Doors musical group mean?
- What is "the mark of the beast?"
- Who is the fallen angel Lucifer?
- What other names does Lucifer go by,, and what does he look like?

- What are the "horsemen of the apocalypse?"

Answers to these mysteries and many more are answered in this book with never-before-seen photos that are truly out of this world.

About the Author

Catholic Mystic and award-winning author and screenwriter Matthew Douglas Pinard is the author of seven books on angels, the afterlife, psychic clairvoyance, prophecy, and miraculous healing.

- Have you ever felt a presence you knew wanted something from you?
- Have you ever felt like you had a gift "locked", which was meant to bring light to this world?
- Have you ever witnessed an actual miracle of healing?
- Have you ever seen what you were convinced was a letter, animal, object, or angel in the skies?
- Are you concerned with the current course the world is on?

Matthew will help you communicate with loved ones who have passed and are angel spirit guides to protect and help us navigate this world.

The author explains his encounter with "The Woman Clothed with the Sun." He became a witness to an amazing precious blood miracle the Vatican is now investigating. It preceded three amazing healing miracles of degenerative diseases among friends and family.

Matthew's photographs will send chills down your spine, proving life exists in other dimensions outside the physical realm. This is a once-in-a-lifetime chance to unlock the deepest mysteries of your own life, bringing this world closer to peace, light, healing, and hope.

Matthew Douglas Pinard (formerly James Douglas Morrison)
734.649.8431 / pinardm@gmail.com / www.jimsnewwine.com

Other Books by Author Matthew

matthewpinardauthor.com

Follow Me:

- Goodreads
- Author Central
- YouTube

Screenplay Awards Matthew Douglas Pinard

Official Selection

Bloodstained Indie Film Festival

StoryPros Awards Screenplay Contest

Military Script Showcase

L.A. Neo Noir Novel Film & Script Festival

True Story International Film Festival

Reel Heart International Film Festival

Hollywood Boulevard International Film Festival

Independent Talents International Film Festival

Fort Worth Indie Film Showcase

California Independent Film Festival

San Pedro International Film Festival,

Southeastern International Film Festival

Louisiana International Film Festival

Official Selection

First Ten Pages Script Contest

Atlanta Comedy Film Festival

Georgia Shorts Film Festival

Official Finalist

Las Vegas International Film and Screenwriting Contest, Honorable Mention

Depth of Field International Film Festival, Award Winner

Beverly Hills International Film Festival, Silver Winner

Queen Palm International Film Festival, Award Winner

Colorado International Film Festival, Quarter-Finalist

Chicago Screenplay Awards, Quarter-Finalist

NYC International Screenplay Awards, Quarter-Finalist

Atlanta Screenplay Awards, Semi-Finalist

Cordillera International Film Festival, Semi-Finalist

Fade In Awards, Finalist

Breaking Walls Thriller Screenplay Award Winner

Vegas Movie Awards,

The Santa Barbara International Screenplay Awards, Finalist

Miami Screen Play Awards, Quarter-Finalist:

www.ingramcontent.com/pod-product-compliance
Lightning Source LLC
Chambersburg PA
CBHW081352070526
44583CB00020B/2529